Buying & Selling A HOUSE OR FLAT

Daily Mail

Buying & Selling A HOUSE OR FLAT

Howard and Jackie Green

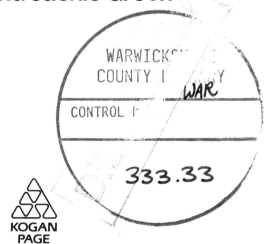

KOGAN
PAGE

First published in Great Britain in 1988 by Kogan Page Limited, 120 Pentonville Road, London N1 9JN

British Library Cataloguing in Publication Data

Green, Howard, *1922-*
    Buying and selling a house or flat.
    1. Great Britain. Houses. Purchase & sale — Practical Information
    I. Title   II. Green, Jackie
    643'.12'0941

    ISBN 1–85091–512–1

Printed and bound in Great Britain by
Biddles Ltd, Guildford

Contents

1. Introduction   **7**

Stress and house purchase 8; Why own your own house or flat? 10; The changing pattern of ownership 11; The changing nature of the housing market 12; Other factors influencing house prices 14; Who controls the housing market? 15; Moving abroad 16

2. What Do I Need?   **17**

Property size 17; Heating 20; Types of property available 22; Which one for me? 24; Living in town or country 25; Leasehold or freehold? 26; Buying old or new properties 26; Searching for property 28; Sources of information 29; Buying a council house 31; Sitting tenants 31

3. Looking at Property   **33**

Inspecting properties 33; Tell-tales in your structural assessment 37; Structural surveys 39; Buying older property 42; Can I afford to buy? 43

4. The Formalities of Buying   **47**

1. Make an offer 47; 2. Notify your agents and advisers 52; 3. Put your own property on the market 58; 4. The interim period 62; 5. The legal process 64; 6. The formalities of buying in Scotland 72

5. Financing Your Purchase   **75**

Mortgages 75; Different types of mortgage 82; Which type of mortgage? 89; How much can I borrow? 90; Tax and tax relief 93; Finance and the first-time buyer 94; Obtaining your mortgage 94

6. Completing the Purchase and Moving   **97**

Insurance 98; Rates 98; Informing people of your move 99; Curtains and carpets 102; Modifications 102; Completing the purchase 103; Moving 103

7. Insurance and Related Issues   **115**

Insuring the structure 115; Specialist insurance 122; Insuring the contents 122; Cover during removal and storage 125; Insurance associated with mortgages and finance 125; Paying for insurance 126

8. Selling Your House or Flat   **129**
Using an estate agent or doing it yourself 129; The DIY
approach 129; The estate agent approach 133; Showing
viewers around 136; Dealing with offers 138; Auctioning
your property 139; Selling in Scotland 140

9. Modifying and Extending Property   **143**
Settling in jobs 143; Major works 146; Raising finance 150;
Getting work done 150; Getting permission 151; What kind
of development to consider 153; What extensions cost 155

Appendices
1. Costs of Installing and Running a Heating System   159
2. Useful Addresses   161
3. Sitting Tenants: The Right to Buy   167
4. Checklist of Fixtures and Fittings Included in a Sale   171
5. Who to Inform of Your New Address   173
6. Calculating the Value of the Contents of Your Property   175
7. Mortgage Comparisons   177
8. How to Advertise   179

Index of Advertisers   **183**

Index   **185**

Chapter 1

Introduction

People buy and sell houses for a variety of reasons. Couples and single people set up home for the first time. A job change necessitates a move from one part of the country to another, as may company relocation. A new baby in the family means space is short and an additional bedroom is required. Elderly parents or relatives are no longer able to look after themselves and come to join the family. Children grow up and move away leaving what was once a well-used property feeling empty and too big. Advancing years mean that the garden is too large to cope with. Death of a husband or wife late in life may necessitate a move to smaller or sheltered accommodation. Financial circumstances change leading to being under-mortgaged, or redundancy means that a smaller mortgage is necessary.

Whatever the cause, buying and selling a house or flat and moving home is a major event for many reasons.

- The purchase of a house or flat represents for most people the largest financial transaction and commitment of their lives. Overheads such as rates, heating, lighting, maintenance and insurance, when added to mortgage payments, make house or flat purchase a major financial item.
- A house is more than just bricks and mortar. It is a home for the occupants and must satisfy their needs both immediately and in the longer term.
- The surrounding area must be able to offer both the social and commercial facilities which are important to modern living. Immediate social contacts, such as neighbours, are important in everyday life.

Whatever the specific reason for buying, selling and moving house, the process is almost invariably associated with major changes in lifestyle or personal circumstances. The burden of moving house, added to these other changes, frequently makes the process stressful, even for the most experienced house-movers.

Stress and house purchase

Everyone involved in the buying and selling of houses and the associated moving will experience some stress during the process. The recognition and acceptance of this fact is the first element in minimising its adverse effects. Different people will be stressed in different ways. For adults the stress may be caused by financial worries and uncertainties. For junior members of a family it may be the result of having to change school or lose contact with friends. The interaction of these two groups will itself cause stress. The two major sources of stress are likely to be related to uncertainty and risk.

- Uncertainty may be caused, among other things, by:
    pressure from other vendors and purchasers;
    delays in searches, contracts or the arrival of the removal firm;
    dilatoriness of the professionals in the process;
    suitability of new schools or jobs, of area and house;
    possibility of defects in property as yet not identified;
    new neighbours.

- Risk:
    Can the property be afforded?
    What if the structure causes problems?
    Will furniture get lost or damaged in the move?

This book shows how to reduce the risks and uncertainties and hence make purchase a less stressful experience.

There are one or two points which are worth emphasising at the outset as they relate to the entire sale and purchase process and should be kept at the back of your mind throughout.

- Involve all affected members of the household or family

in the process of purchase and movement. This is particularly important for people with children.

- Anticipate problems and delays; they always arise, especially delays.
- Know what questions to ask; write them down if necessary, *and listen to the answers.*
- *Do not be fobbed off by the professionals.* If they are truly professional they will listen.

Having said all this it is well worth asking yourself if the move is absolutely necessary at this precise moment. If the answer is 'Yes', then this book will help you through the potential turmoil. It will give you advice on particular approaches and actions to take and perhaps, most importantly, will provide reassurance that the problems which you encounter are not unique to your move and have been experienced by countless intrepid vendors and purchasers in the past. It is best to avoid moving house while you have other causes for stress, such as illness (your own, or in the family), or death of a close friend or relative.

For some people moving house is a commonplace activity for which a considerable amount of assistance is provided by, for example, employers. For others, it is a once or twice in a lifetime experience for which there is little or no assistance or preparation. In Britain people do not move house as frequently as in the United States, for example. We are not a very mobile population. Evidence suggests that people are increasingly reluctant to be involved even in company moves. Nevertheless, over 40 per cent of owner occupiers have lived in their present houses for less than ten years. As the buying and selling of one's house or flat is associated with the different stages of the life cycle, it is more frequent in the under-thirty age group than any other.

While this book is not intended as a substitute for professional assistance and advice, it will provide an understanding of how to tackle the professionals and enable you to ask meaningful questions with confidence.

Information is presented simply and concisely in a fashion which will allow the reader to put together his or her own strategy. Every house or flat, every individual's need or want, and every house moving, is unique. There is no absolute right or wrong way to buy or sell property. There are, however, broad pathways which can be followed. This book is about those pathways. Where possible lists and checklists are used to enable the reader to put together a personal moving package. As many of the lists may be needed separately, they are presented as appendices.

Why own your own house or flat?

If you already own your own home then perhaps the question does not arise. For many people it is well worth considering. There are both advantages and disadvantages to ownership. Some of these are listed below, not in any specific order or importance.

Advantages:
- much greater choice of property;
- more possible locations;
- choice of public and private facilities, such as shops and schools;
- security of tenure;
- a traditional hedge against inflation;
- mortgage tax relief;
- freedom to modify and decorate to personal taste.

Disadvantages:
- responsibility of ownership for items such as rates, repairs and maintenance;
- financial burden of mortgage finance and uncertainty of interest rate changes.

For most people the advantages far outweigh the disadvantages and home ownership has become a major political issue since 1979. However, for some people, particularly the elderly and first-time buyers, the advantages may appear to be a long way away. The ever increasing burden of repairs and maintenance has created problems for the large number of elderly people who own their homes. This factor alone is a major issue which must be assessed in the criteria of choice outlined in Chapter 2.

The argument for home ownership requires a long-term view of costs which, at the outset of one's working life, can be difficult to accept. In 1985, for example, the average weekly expenditure on housing, including mortgage, rates and insurance, for those in the process of purchase, was £47.84, while for local authority tenants the figure was £14.48. In the long term, these figures will change as inflation raises rent payments and reduces the real value of mortgage repayments. For owner occupiers who had finished paying off their mortgage in 1985, average weekly expenditure was only £13.68.

It is important to recognise that financial problems can arise in house purchase and that as a result families can be forced out of ownership by the banks and building societies. Of the 6.7 million building society loans outstanding in 1985, 11,400 were in arrears of more than 12 months. In the same year the societies repossessed 16,800 properties. Although this is only a small fraction of the number of mortgaged properties, repossession is a personal catastrophe for each individual.

The changing pattern of ownership

Historically, home ownership was the privilege of the affluent, but there has been a dramatic shift in the proportion of owner occupation from 30 per cent of houses in 1951 to 62 per cent in 1985. The position is different in Scotland where, largely for historical reasons, only 40 per cent of property is owner occupied.

Increasing affluence and tax incentives have been major factors contributing to these changes. The Housing Acts of 1980 and 1984 which gave local authority tenants the right to buy their homes at discount greatly increased the sale of both council and new town development corporation houses. Sale numbers rose from 92,000 in 1980 to a peak of 228,000 in 1982 before falling back to 116,000 in 1985. This legislation has given a great boost to the opportunities for the less well off to buy their own homes. Unfortunately, most sales are of houses rather than flats and the opportunities for council flat purchase are much fewer.

Even with these schemes the less well off still find it hard to enter the housing market. In 1985, for example, only 28 per cent of households where the head was earning up to £200 a week were buying their house on mortgage, whereas for those earning over £300 the figure was 74 per cent. Money, as will be seen later, is a key to house or flat purchase. Start saving now!

The changing nature of the housing market

The present pattern in the housing market is influenced by two simple factors, supply and demand.

Despite massive increases in private sector building, there are still major housing shortages in certain parts of the country, especially in London, the South East and East Anglia, where the levels of economic activity have stimulated the need for new housing. Elsewhere the pattern is more confusing. Areas which have suffered industrial decline find themselves with a surplus of housing and many home owners find it difficult if not impossible to sell. This is particularly true in urban areas of the major industrial regions. On the other hand, demand in the outer suburban areas of these regions and in the rural villages is particularly high as the better off try to move away from the problems of city life. These recent increases in housing demand have placed considerable pressure on the authorities to release more land for development. They have also had a major effect on house price changes.

Figures from the Halifax Building Society indicate that there are increasing differences between house prices in different parts of the country and that these are becoming greater. This is shown in Table 1.1. For anyone buying a house for the first

House type	North £	East Midlands £	South East £	Greater London £
Terraced	22,058	24,811	53,048	76,343
Semi-detached	30,452	31,777	65,321	92,058
Detached	51,241	53,542	106,960	147,716
Flats/Maisonettes	17,293	24,194	44,466	62,325

Table 1.1 *Average house prices in England 1987*

time or moving from one part of the country to another, these figures are a stark reminder of the price increases which have taken place over the last few years. In 1987, for example, the Halifax Building Society noted an average price increase of 15 per cent throughout the country, with rises as much as 30 per cent in London, the South East and East Anglia. The average price paid for a house by a first-time buyer rose by over £6,000 in the same period.

The figures conceal major local variations within regional markets caused by local factors. Table 1.2 shows the pattern of price differences within Yorkshire and Humberside, one of the cheapest housing regions of the country.

Town	Price £	Town	Price £
Bradford	26,850	Doncaster	22,850
Grimsby	26,800	Halifax	32,200
Harrogate	38,100	Hull	29,750
Leeds	32,100	Rotherham	25,000
Sheffield	28,350	York	36,750

Table 1.2 *Average semi-detached house prices: Yorkshire and Humberside*

These price changes and the changing patterns of demand, both in terms of location and house type and size, are forcing the house builders themselves to develop new approaches to housing provision. House buyers, particularly in South East England, are having to consider commuting longer and longer distances to obtain housing at reasonable prices.

The house builders are now putting increased pressure on government to allow the release of more land for new housing. While developers and conservationists argue over the use of Green Belt land for housing, the builders are pushing on with ever larger house building schemes. Companies like Consortium Developments, a group of nine major house builders, have put forward new settlement schemes including houses, pubs, shops and schools at locations such as Tillingham Hall in Essex, Foxley Wood in Hampshire, Wilburton near Cambridge, and Stone Bassett, some seven miles east of Oxford. A similar development is currently being planned at Wetherby in West Yorkshire.

Development in the so-called inner city areas offers the other end of the spectrum of housing initiatives. The London Docklands is perhaps the best known focus of new city centre housing development. Here the major house builders such as Barratt and Wimpey have built houses and maisonettes and have converted the former warehouses into sophisticated flats. To a lesser extent the same process is taking place in other cities.

The range of house types being built is now widening, making more housing opportunities available to the purchaser, in theory at least. The standard three bedroom semi-detached is a thing of the past as land prices and consumer choice force designers and builders to consider alternatives. Accommodation for smaller families and childless couples features more widely in new developments as do single room studios for the young single person. Houses are now on the market which can easily be extended. One major builder's housing developments cater specifically for the changing requirements of the individual's life cycle: studios, one and two bedroom houses, and detached larger houses, all on the same site. More retirement accommodation is being built in special complexes where elderly people can live in flats around communal amenities.

All these types of development reflect market adjustments to the changing pattern of housing demand and particularly the changing structure of the population.

Other factors influencing house prices

In addition to the broad regional patterns of house prices a range of more detailed factors influence price. These will become clear to any house purchaser or vendor.

- *Size of property*. This is the basic yardstick by which valuations are made: simple square footage of the property followed by number of rooms.
- *Type of property*. Terraced, semi-detached, detached.
- *Accommodation offered*. Number of bathrooms, reception rooms, sizes of particular rooms such as kitchens, garages.
- *Basic condition of property*. Level of repair and maintenance.
- *Standard of fittings,* particularly in bathrooms and kitchens.

Houses of similar size and standard can vary markedly in price between different areas of the same town. All towns have their sought-after areas because of standards of local schools or services, pleasantness of the locality or simply because of a 'good address'. Prices will also be influenced by local supply and demand for specific types of property at a particular time.

Who controls the housing market?

It is important to realise that, as in any area of commerce, there are several major interest groups who to a greater or lesser extent, control what goes on. These groups will be referred to again in subsequent chapters but they are noted below. When consulting or referring to any of the organisations or individuals you should be aware that they represent a particular interest and that their advice will be influenced by this.

Central government
- Major housing policies.
- Housing finance.
- Housing improvement policy.
- Housing land policy.
- Major planning issues.

Local government
- The detailed implementation of central government policies.
- Land allocation.
- Administration of improvement grants and schemes.
- Council housing.

The property professions
- *Architects.* Design and layout of housing. Improvements and house extensions.
- *Chartered surveyors.* Valuations of property, property management, structural and valuation surveys.
- *Estate agents.* Valuation of property. Negotiation and selling of property. Increasingly dealing with complete relocation packages. Housing finance.
- *House builders.* Companies who do the actual construction work.
- *Banks and building societies.* Housing finance on both

personal and developer scale.
- *Insurance companies.* Companies involved in the financing and development of housing, and particularly flats.

While each of these groups consists of a range of companies of all sizes, the tendency is for all groups to become larger and consequently more powerful in the marketplace. Also, organisations with different interests tend to group together to offer a range of services. This is particularly the case with the insurance companies and building societies who are taking an increasingly dominant role in the housing market.

Moving abroad

This book does not attempt to advise on buying and selling properties overseas. Readers are referred to three relevant titles published by Kogan Page: *Living and Retiring Abroad* by Michael Furnell (second edition 1987); *Timesharing: A Buyer's Guide* by James Edmonds (1988); and *Working Abroad: the Daily Telegraph Guide* by Godfrey Golzen (eleventh edition 1988).

Chapter 2
What Do I Need?

Let us now take a closer look at the factors which should be taken into account when setting out in search of a new house or flat.

It is essential to identify at the outset individual housing needs, both present and future. In identifying your needs you may find it useful to draw up a checklist of factors on the lines of those below.

Property size

When considering space requirements and the number and size of rooms that you need, it is important to look to the future as well as at the present.

It is likely that elderly relatives will visit more frequently?
Will the children be leaving home in the near future?
Are you about to start your own business and need an office?

While it is impossible to cover all eventualities, careful assessment of present and future needs is a vital element of the choice process.

Number of rooms

Reception rooms
How many reception rooms, dining room, sitting room, drawing room, study, do you have at present?
Are they adequate?
Have you too many?
What will future needs be?
Where will the children do their homework when they grow up?

Where will junior practise his trumpet?
Will the reception rooms be open plan or separated?
Is the need for privacy an important consideration?

Bedrooms
How many do you have at present?
Will the family or household be growing or contracting?
What about elderly relatives or visitors?
Will growing children need a room of their own?

Kitchen
Is the kitchen just a place where you cook or do you need a kitchen diner?
Where do the washing machine and tumble drier currently go?
Would it be useful to have a separate utility room or laundry?

Bathroom
Do you need two bathrooms or would it simply be a luxury to have two?
Larger households find two bathrooms ease the congestion in the early morning rush.
Would an additional shower room solve the problem?

Toilets
How many do you need?
Should they be separate from the bathroom or not?
Those households with young or elderly members should consider the need for a cloakroom with toilet on the ground floor.

Size of rooms
It is useful to have some ideas on the maximum and minimum size of rooms which you need before you begin looking for property. It is very easy to be carried away in individual properties by rooms which are simply not big enough.

Make a list of all the large, awkward items of furniture. What size room do you need for the grand piano, the grandfather clock or the oak sideboard?

Remember to measure and include ceiling heights: particularly when moving from older to newer property, differences in ceiling height can be a problem. Large rooms are very useful but they can be expensive to heat.

Is a large kitchen necessary?
Do you wish to be able to eat in the kitchen too?

Perhaps halls and stairways are not so important but it is useful to note minimum sizes here too. It is not unusual to find the lounge suite, piano or wardrobe getting stuck on a staircase or halfway between hall and drawing room. Narrow halls can lead to congestion getting in and out. A wide hall and entrance will be a useful parking place for prams.

Garage and car parking space

Do you need a garage with the added facility to store tools etc or is car parking space adequate?
Would on-street parking space satisfy your parking needs? Most insurance companies charge higher premiums for cars inadequately garaged.
Think of future needs. How long will it be before other members of the household have cars of their own?
Where you will park the boat or caravan?

Garden

The house with a garden seems to be the traditional ideal. If you have a garden at present, is it about the right size? What use do you make of it? While a large garden may sound attractive in principle, do remember that the lawns will have to be cut! Even with the modern equipment gardening does take time. Where will you keep the equipment which you will need to maintain the garden?

If you are getting on in years it is worth thinking of the liabilities of a large garden. Moving to a house with a garden may be a desirable goal for those with young families living in cities.

Having made a list of the basic attributes of the houses or flats you wish to search for, you should look at the more detailed aspects of your needs. Here again it is worth assessing your current property (of parents or friends, if you are buying for the first time) and itemise the strengths and weaknesses. The items you might consider include:

Number and distribution of electric power points;

Position of doors in rooms;
Position, orientation and size of windows;
Relationship of different rooms (the distance of the kitchen from the dining room, for example);
Layout of kitchen;
Source of heating.

Heating

Heating is worthy of some consideration at this stage of the process.

What type of heating do you have at present?
Is it good, adequate or inadequate for your needs?

Central heating

If you have central heating at present and are convinced of its merits then the costs of installation in a house without it would need thorough investigation at the outset. If you do not have central heating, now is the time to consider its advantages and disadvantages.

Advantages	Disadvantages
Gives greater use of all space	Cost of installation
Is flexible in time terms	Dryness of atmosphere
Can be controlled automatically	Costs of maintenance

There are several different types of central heating systems and it is worth considering the main points of each. Most people tend to look for the systems with which they are familiar: it is worth keeping an open mind. An indication of the installation and running costs of different systems is given in Appendix 4.

Gas central heating

Small and standard bore water circulation and radiators. These are the most common systems. They are very flexible and this flexibility can be increased by the use of individual room thermostats or thermostatic valves. They need regular maintenance.

Usually the system will include an independently controllable water heating system.

Hot air ducted systems. This form of heating is normally only installed when a house is built, as the ducting would damage the structure subsequently. In these systems hot air is ducted around the house and into rooms through vents located in the floor, in walls or set into ceilings. This is a very immediate form of central heating which needs similar maintenance to the water system. Hot air systems do not suffer from leaks. They are less easy to control on a room-by-room basis although vents can be opened and closed manually.

The major disadvantage of these systems is that they collect and redistribute household dust in spite of filters, and are consequently not recommended for those with chest or breathing problems or allergies.

You will need a separate water heating system.

Electric central heating
This is usually in the form of night storage heaters which heat up during the night, using cheap rate electricity (Economy Seven), and release the heat slowly during the day. The heaters are connected to a special electricity circuit. The image of the night storage heater is changing and modern units are extremely efficient and neat. The systems do not allow the temperature control and flexibility of the gas systems.

They require separate water heating systems which can be linked to the cheap rate electricity.

Other sources of heating
Even in houses with central heating it is often necessary or useful to provide additional heat sources. While breaks in the gas supply are very rare, electricity cuts are more frequent, as many people were made aware in the latter part of 1987. Most of the controls on central heating systems rely on electricity. For many people, particularly the elderly who need higher room temperatures, central heating is best used as a background heat source in conjunction with another more direct source.

Gas fires. An efficient form of room heating. Take care with the coal-effect type, however: they may look attractive, but most of the heat goes up the chimney. Regular maintenance is important. Rooms should be well ventilated to avoid risks from carbon monoxide fumes.

Balanced flue wall heaters are a very useful way of bringing extra heat to halls and landings. They need to be mounted on an outside wall.

Portable bottled gas fires are an increasingly popular form of room heating. They offer the advantage of low capital costs for purchase and portability. The bottled gas, which is now widely available, can frequently be delivered free, hence avoiding the major drawback to this form of heating. You will need to check in your lease that gas canisters are not prohibited in your building, if you are a flat-dweller.

Electric fires. A wide variety of electric heaters is now marketed to solve space heating problems. While they produce immediate and flexible heat at quite low capital cost, they do have high running costs.

Open fires. Having lost ground in the post-war period as central heating gained in popularity, coal fires are becoming increasingly popular as a form of space heating. Many of the associated inconveniences such as ash disposal are being minimised in modern appliances which are capable of burning a variety of fuels. The coal fire and chimney fulfil a vital role in providing ventilation in a house.

A range of other fuel sources is available for domestic heating. Peat and wood burning equipment is popular in certain parts of the country. Where fuel is readily available these sources can be very satisfactory. As with any open hearth system, it is important to check that there are no 'clean air' regulations in force.

Types of property available

Residential property is subdivided into five broad categories.

Terraced houses

As the term suggests, several units are joined together to make up a terrace. There is an enormous variation in the size and character of terraced property, from the Georgian terraces in Bath to the terraces of workers' cottages in some industrial cities.

In general, terraced property is smaller than other types and is cheaper when outside fashionable areas. Terraced houses usually have small gardens, often only to the rear. End terraces are frequently larger, some with large corner plot gardens. Terraced houses are usually cheaper to heat because of the smaller number of external walls. Noise can be a problem. When terraced houses are referred to as 'town houses', they are usually on three floors.

Semi-detached houses
Semi-detached property is perhaps the most popular type of property in Britain. The three-bedroom 'semi' of the interwar period is still built today. More recently builders have introduced variations in terms of sizes and number of rooms. The garden is the great advantage of the semi over the terraced property, along with the garage or at least access and space for a garage.

Detached houses
Increasing affluence in the last 15 years has led to the current popularity of this type of property. Terms such as 'executive' have crept in to emphasise the image and status of detached living. The modern detached house typically has four bedrooms and a double garage. Older detached property is frequently much larger.

Bungalows
A bungalow is a property in which most if not all the accommodation is on the ground floor. It may be detached or semi-detached. It was popular in the post-war period, particularly in the Midlands and North, but rising land prices are greatly reducing the number now built. The bungalow is particularly appropriate for the less agile, and properties purpose-built for the elderly are often of this type.

Bungalows have the advantage of easy external maintenance. (Little need to use ladders.) The disadvantage is the cost of heating where every room has two outside walls.

Flats and maisonettes
These are usually accommodation which is part of a larger building. They may be developed by subdivision of an existing

building or be purpose-built. Flats have shared stairways and access and sometimes communal gardens. Maisonettes have their own entrances and stairways. Both flats and maisonettes share maintenance funded from a service charge. In blocks of flats, the service charge may also cover central heating and/or hot water, entryphone, porterage and/or security services. There can be restrictions involved in flat living, such as no pets.

There is a growing variety of accommodation available which does not fall neatly into the classification. Much of this is developed for particular groups: disabled people, the single person, the newly married couple and the elderly.

While most of the property types mentioned are purpose built, some will be converted from existing buildings such as mills, railway buildings, schools, chapels and barns.

Which one for me?

The particular type of property which you search for will reflect your needs and ability to pay. If you have a large growing family then a large detached house will be the answer. If you are single then a flat may be just for you. Moving from one type of property to another poses problems.

If moving to a flat from a house you will need to consider:
- space for your furniture (and whether you have to dispose of some, or even buy anew);
- access, if not on ground floor;
- specific requirements and restrictions imposed by the lease;
- coping without a garden;
- the idiosyncrasies of your neighbours' personalities, noises and smells;
- others being aware of your habits (loud music, kitchen smells);
- adjusting to shared areas and garden.

If moving from a flat to a house you will need to consider:
- increased costs, such as heating and insurance;
- responsibility for getting repairs done;
- more cleaning and general maintenance;

- the problems and cost of finding adequate furniture and carpets;
- finding time for the garden and providing the appropriate tools.

All these issues can be resolved and most people adjust to the new type of living. It is wise to keep them in mind when you look at property.

Living in town or country

Increasingly, people are moving into suburban and rural locations. For some this is a necessity imposed by employment and for others it is the only way of finding property at a reasonable price. Commuting distances in the South East are becoming longer as people live in distant rural and semi-rural areas. The idyllic rural setting may create its own problems, so consider some of the following issues.

- It may be delightful in the summer but consider access problems in winter.
- There may be a limited range of housing available.
- Some services may not be available (gas, electricity, mains sewage) and others may be at a great distance (doctors, dentists, schools, hospitals).
- There may be limited public transport.
- Fewer local social and educational facilities may be available.
- Planning restrictions, such as Green Belt, may limit any development of the property.
- Rural smells can become tiresome.
- Roads may be congested with tourists.

Some people simply do not fit into a rural environment and in small villages in particular may have difficulty in being accepted by local people.

Urban living has its own advantages and disadvantages:

- a greater range of housing available;
- easier access to a wide range of services including schools and medical facilities;

- more convenient shopping with wider choice and lower prices;
- wider range of entertainment and social activities;
- crowded, polluted environment;
- higher house prices;
- higher insurance rates for items such as house contents and car;
- feeling of isolation.

Leasehold or freehold?

Property is held in two types of tenure: either leasehold or freehold.

Leasehold property ultimately returns to the ownership of the lessor when the lease expires – usually after 99 or 999 years. As the unexpired period of the lease gets shorter this may affect the value of the property. However, the Leasehold Reform Act of 1967, with some exceptions, gives owners of leasehold houses the right to buy their freehold. The lease will include covenants which are the terms on which the property is leased. These covenants may be restrictive, preventing activities which are important to you. In flats the lease will detail the terms of any service agreements and charges. Lease-holders pay an annual ground rent to the landlord.

Freehold property is held in absolute ownership with no involvement or commitment of other parties. This is the most common form of tenure in England, Scotland and Wales.

Buying old or new properties

Whether you buy a new house, second-hand but modern, or older house, or a flat in a new purpose-built block or in a conversion, is a matter of personal preference. Your housing needs may allow you little choice – few are the modern houses which have room for a grand piano or snooker table! There are some general points which may influence your decision.

New houses

The purchase of a new house:

- may allow your own personal needs to be incorporated

during construction;
- will normally include a 10-year National House Building Council (NHBC) guarantee;
- will make it easier to obtain a mortgage;
- will require little decoration and maintenance for several years;
- will allow you to become part of the community from the outset;
- may allow you to inspect a show house or flat before making a decision to buy;
- will give you some choice in kitchen and bathroom fittings.

But:

- it may be difficult to resell before the entire development is complete, and this sometimes takes years;
- it may be some time before local bus services are routed near new housing estates;
- the development may remain a building site for some time with associated muddy roads and paths, and noise of contractors' equipment;
- the property will probably need fixtures and fittings – cupboards to curtain rails (some new houses come completely fitted with curtains, carpets, fridge and washing machine etc, but do not forget that these items are all included in the purchase price and may lead to problems with resale values – unlike the property itself, consumer items will depreciate very quickly);
- the garden will need laying out, paths and patios constructing and huts and greenhouses erecting (all take time and money).

Second-hand property
The major advantage is that most of the hard work has been done already. Gardens are laid out, curtain rails installed. Prices are negotiable, especially if they include carpets, fixtures and fittings.

Problems may include:

- decorations which do not suit;

- poor decorative order;
- movement may involve a 'chain' of buyers and sellers;
- difficulties of moving into an existing established neighbourhood.

Older property

Buying older property poses some risks but does usually allow you to purchase property of character. The major advantages are the peculiarities brought by long occupation and change and large proportions, particularly of room sizes and ceiling heights.

Problems may include:

- structural defects;
- decoration;
- difficulty in borrowing money;
- lack of modern amenities.

Searching for property

By now you will have a reasonably precise idea of your housing requirements. No mention has yet been made of the costs. Clearly this is an important element of the decision process and will be discussed in detail in Chapter 3.

The strategy you adopt in your search will be broadly similar whether you are moving a long distance from familiar surroundings or looking in your home town. The differences are largely due to lack of familiarity and time. Moving into an area for the first time involves a complete learning process. You will need information on a range of key issues from good schools and reliable estate agents to the good areas in which to live. To acquire this information and search for property takes time. For these reasons it is wise, if at all possible, to become completely familiar with the area before buying. This may involve renting property before finally selecting a house or flat to buy.

If you are forced to buy immediately, then consider using one of the house relocation agencies (see Appendix 2 for the address of the Association of Relocation Agents) or use one of the agents operating the National Homelink Service.

Sources of information

There are five major sources of information which you should consider when looking for property. These are estate agents, the press, the new homes hot line, friends and personal search of billboards.

Estate agents

All towns have their estate agents, usually located in close proximity to one another. Agencies can either be the small single town agent or the larger regional or national agency. Some agencies deal with districts of towns and cities. Most will deal with residential property; some may not include converted or older property. Remember that agents act on behalf of the vendor. This will influence any negotiations you may have and most certainly affects the language used in the particulars of property. While agents must not misrepresent property, you will soon become familiar with the euphemisms adopted.

Ask to be put on the agent's mailing list to receive particulars of specific properties and the property guides which many agents now produce regularly. Tell the agent exactly what you are looking for so that only potential properties are sent. Agents frequently group property in price bands, £50,000–£75,000, £75,000–£100,000, for example. Do not be discouraged if they send property which is priced above your upper limit. It may indicate that it is worth making an offer. Do not be tempted to offer above what you have designated your upper limit, but make sure that you have not set your upper limit too low. One or two thousand pounds more may make a lot of difference and enable you to buy the property you really want.

Buying through a good agent does have many advantages. The agent will be anxious for you to purchase (his fee or commission depends on it) and hence the agent should help in the process of purchase. Agents often act as a building society agency and will be able to arrange a mortgage. Ask colleagues and friends which agencies they have used and which they can recommend.

The press

Local, regional and national press advertise property for sale.

Additionally, there are a number of specialist weekly magazines such as *Exchange and Mart, Daltons Weekly* and the *London and Weekly Advertiser* which cover property. Those looking for a country mansion might care to consult *Country Life* or the *Tatler*. In most towns the local press is a useful source of information. The property page, which usually appears regularly on a particular day, will give you a very good overview of the local market as well as identifying specific property.

It is worth considering placing an advert in the 'property wanted' sections too. You may be able to negotiate a lower price for property as the vendor will not be paying an agent's commission.

New homes hot line

The New Homes Marketing Board has set up a hot line which will provide you with information about new houses in your search area. The hot line is open from 9 am to 5.15 pm on weekdays and from 10 am to 4 pm on Saturdays on 01-935 7464. If you give brief details of the type of property you are looking for, the service will provide you with a list of suitable properties. The service is computerised and is kept up to date.

Friends and colleagues

Consult friends and colleagues about your housing needs. Particularly when moving into a new area, they can be a useful source of information. By developing a network it is often possible to find property before it comes on to the market formally. It is best to pay an agreed valuation price. If the vendor finds he has sold too cheaply, he may pull out of the deal at an inconvenient moment.

Personal search

Simply driving around your search area is likely to provide you with possible properties. Billboards are designed to catch the eye and can be a very effective way of advertising property. Many agents' boards indicate that viewing is by appointment only. While there may be a minority of vendors who would take exception to a chance visit, most are only too keen to sell the property. Knock on the door, you have nothing to lose.

Buying a council house

It has been assumed so far that you will be looking for a house to buy. As a sitting tenant you may, however, be considering buying the house you currently rent from one of the public bodies identified in Appendix 3.

Normally you have the right to buy your house or flat if:

- you rent your home from one of the landlords named in Appendix 3;
- you have spent at least two years as a tenant of any of the landlords named in Appendix 3;
- the property is a separate dwelling.

There are a few exceptions to these broad rules which include:

- housing specifically developed for the elderly, disabled or mentally handicapped;
- housing which is being used as temporary accommodation;
- some lettings to people who are employed by the landlord.

As a sitting tenant you will be eligible for a discount on the sale price. This discount may be as much as £35,000. To qualify for a discount you simply add up the total number of years you have been a tenant of either group of landlords shown in Appendix 3. The basic discount after a qualifying tenancy of two years is 32 per cent for a house and 44 per cent for a flat. For each additional year of qualifying tenancy you gain 1 per cent additional discount up to a maximum of 60 per cent for a house, and 2 per cent for a flat up to a maximum of 70 per cent.

Table 2.1 gives examples of the discounts available.

Sitting tenants

If you are a sitting tenant and are considering buying your house or flat, a useful leaflet, *Your Right to Buy your Home* is produced by the Department of the Environment and Welsh Office. This, and the form *Notice Claiming the Right to Buy* (Form RTB1), is also available from the local authority housing department or a Citizens Advice Bureau. Both these organisations will be able to help you further.

| Qualifying period | Discount | |
Years	Houses %	Flats and maisonettes %
2	32	44
5	35	50
10	40	60
15	45	70
20	50	70
25	55	70
30	60	70
Over 30	60	70

Table 2.1 *Discounts available for public sector housing purchasers*

Should you wish to consider buying a property which has a sitting tenant, it is essential to find out the terms of the lease and to know what the tenant's contribution is to maintenance and general expenses. A crucial point might be whether the Rent Acts would permit the rent to be increased. It is often difficult to obtain a mortgage on property with a sitting tenant; this, as well as the condition of the property, will affect the price.

Chapter 3
Looking at Property

Armed with the estate agent's information, the checklist of items included in your 'needs' list and a tape measure you are ready to visit potential houses or flats. Quite often the agent will insist on visiting the property with you, having made an appointment for you to view. If you are lucky you may be able to visit alone. In cases where the property is unoccupied some agents will simply loan the keys at your convenience. While the presence of the agent may be useful to answer detailed questions, the first visit to a property is best done alone so that the initial impressions can be discussed freely.

Inspecting properties

First impressions are important. It is not unusual to get no further than parking briefly in the road outside. Some houses are simply not suitable. Once inside keep an open mind. Many of the impressions of properties are given by decoration that is not to one's taste, poor decoration and strange layouts. You have to imagine living in the house or flat. If you do not feel easy or feel that you do not fit, then perhaps this is not the house for you. On the other hand, if the first impression is positive and you feel that the house provides you with most of your needs, then it is worth looking at in more detail.

Do not be pressured by the agent. Take time to make up your mind at this early stage. The agent will wait. He will make a considerable amount of money if he sells the property to you.

If first impressions are good, then a detailed look is called for. You may find it appropriate to have a checklist of questions to ask yourself and possibly the vendor and agent. The broad factors to investigate will relate to the following conditions.

- *Suitability in terms of size.* Do not be tempted to purchase a property which is either too big, too small or of different general proportions from what you want. It is very easy to be attracted by larger property. Remember it has to be heated and cleaned. Check that the garage is large enough to take your car and there is room to open the doors.
- *Situation.* While some degree of flexibility in situation may be fine, a north- and east-facing property will be darker and more expensive to heat than a south- and west-facing one.
- *Location.* Are there any farms or factories nearby which emit unpleasant odours?
- *Layout.* Are the rooms appropriately laid out? Simple issues such as having to pass through a dining room to get to the kitchen may seem trivial at first but can become a permanent irritation.
- *Heating.* Is the property centrally heated? Is the system modern? It is often as expensive to replace or modify an existing system as it is to install from scratch.
- *Condition.* Is the property in a reasonable state of repair and in reasonable decorative order? Do not expect a property to be in immaculate decorative order. It might indicate that something is being concealed if it is.
- *Garden.* Is the garden an appropriate size? Neither compromise your needs nor underestimate the time involved in taming an overgrown garden.

On your visit take notes and, if necessary, draw simple diagrams of layout. These will allow you to discuss the property more easily afterwards. Most people find it impossible to remember every aspect of a house after only one visit. Simple facts such as the relative layout of rooms and position of doors can easily be forgotten.

If you are attracted to a particular property, make a second visit and look in more detail. It is worth making a second visit on a different day of the week and at a different time of the day. Very different impressions can be gained of property at different times. Between five and seven in the evening will give you a good indication of the traffic levels in the vicinity. Morning and afternoon visits will allow you to assess the levels of natural light available and the general brightness of the property.

Ask the vendors to indicate exactly what is included in the sale and what is not. When visiting a furnished house it is very difficult to identify what are fixtures and what are not. Do not be embarrassed to use a checklist such as that given in Appendix 4. Some people strip the property bare when they sell, often leaving only exposed wires where those attractive wall lamps were found or no light bulbs in other fittings. It is always wise to assume nothing rather than be shocked later.

It may be useful to ask what will be going, too. Although your solicitor will negotiate compensation for the removal of the garage full of junk, the hassle is better avoided.

It is important on these visits to establish if all the services within the house work properly. Try all the taps and flush the loo. Switch on extractor fans. Check that the electric points are not damaged and are all in working order. In older property check the general state of the electric installation. Has the property been rewired? Ask a competent electrician to check the wiring. The mains plug circuits should be three-pin 13 amp. Lighting circuits are more difficult to assess. However, if the switches are of the old-fashioned round type or the flex is of the spiral variety, the chances are that the system will need rewiring. This is not necessarily a major problem and is something which can be used in price negotiation.

If the house is centrally heated ask for a demonstration of the system. Check the age of the system too. Older systems can be troublesome. The age of the boiler is perhaps the most important thing to check. Look out for rusty marks on radiators, too. They often indicate leaks. However, older systems are no longer the risk they used to be, as British Gas have recently introduced a maintenance contract which covers central heating systems comprehensively regardless of age.

In the case of houses, the number of storeys or the height can be an important factor for maintenance and repair to items such as the roof. Costs rise significantly in three storey and higher property, as scaffolding and additional insurance are required. Bungalows are clearly at a premium in such instances.

Flats and maisonettes
If you are buying a flat or maisonette there are factors which you should bear in mind.

- *Layout.* You may look at basement, ground floor and upper floor flats. Each has its advantages and disadvantages. Assess each for your personal circumstances.
  Is the room layout sensible? How far is the kitchen from the front door for rubbish disposal? Is there a rubbish chute?
  Does the main room double up as a corridor?
  Is the room arrangement appropriate for sound intrusion? Will the shared spaces such as stairs and landings create noise problems?
- *Outside.* Is there a communal garden? Who maintains it? Is it well kept?
  Is there adequate garaging and parking space? How far is it from the front door? Is there room to park prams and pushchairs?
- *Services.* What is the source of heating? Is it communal or individual? If communal, how is it charged?
  Is mail delivered directly to your door or to a central point? Is there a porterage or security service? How is this paid for?
- *Outgoings.* Who is responsible for:
  – Insurance of the structure.
  – Repair and maintenance of the property including lifts, halls, stairways and roof.
  – Redecoration.
  – Gardens and external communal spaces.
  – Exterior/interior decoration. When is it due and how is it funded?
- *Lease.* How many years are left of the lease?
  What are the terms of the lease?
  What does the lease say about maintenance and service charges?

An excellent booklet *Buying a Flat? Don't Buy a Lifetime of Problems as Well,* is produced by the Royal Institution of Chartered Surveyors and the Law Society.

Take a careful look at the overall structure of the house or flat both inside and out. While it may be necessary to have a professional survey undertaken eventually, a lot of time and expense can be saved by careful personal inspection. You are bound to find some problems. If you identify several it may be wise to think again. If in doubt, ask a local builder to come along and look over the property and give a rough estimate for wise to think again. If in doubt, ask a local builder to come along and look over the property and give a rough estimate for the work required.

Problems identified in a flat might indicate that the terms of the lease which should normally include a fund for repairs and maintenance are not being adhered to. The joint ownership of such property can mean that it is difficult to get repairs carried out.

Tell-tales in your structural assessment

Inside

- Look for stains on ceilings in upper floor rooms, especially around ceiling roses, as this will usually indicate roof problems.
- Check ceilings under valleys on the roof for damp stains.
- Is any ceiling paper loose and discoloured?
- Are ceilings bulging or badly cracked? Remember that in modern houses regular shaped cracks are often found where plaster has dried out around plaster boards. This does not usually present a major repair problem.
- Bulging downstairs ceilings can indicate problems with floor joists above. Again, remember that in older property some sagging may be inevitable.
- Look at the skirting boards. Cracks between the boards and the walls may indicate structural movement.
- Loose wallpaper above the skirting can indicate rising damp.
- Look at the timbers carefully for any signs of woodworm or rot.

Outside

Look at the general state of the outside fabric, specifically, the roof and walls.

The roof

- Are any tiles missing?
- Are the ridge tiles well cemented?
- Are the chimney pots well cemented?
- Are the valley gutters in good condition? Is there any sign of patching of the valleys?

If necessary take a pair of binoculars to help in your examination of the roof. Compare it with others nearby.

Walls
- Look carefully for bulges and cracks. In mining areas or where settlement problems are known, make a careful note of these. They may be very old problems and no longer an active issue.
- Check for damp patches on walls – green mould etc.
- Take a careful look at the damp course. In pre-First World War houses there may be no damp course. In modern housing the damp course is at least 6 inches above the ground level all round the property. Even in new houses it is not unusual to see paths and gardens built above the level of the damp course – a sure way to get rising damp.
- If it is raining when you visit go outside and look at the guttering and down pipes and check for leaks.

If your assessment of the structural condition of the property suggests that there may be some problems and you are still keen to buy, it may be worth considering a full structural survey. If the vendors have lived in the property for only a few years it may be worth asking if they had a survey undertaken and ask to see it. The problems which you identify may have been identified at the earlier time by the previous purchaser's survey. This may indicate that they are no longer serious enough to warrant action.

Damp and wood treatment surveys

Whether you have a structural survey or not it is worth having damp and wood treatment surveys undertaken. Contact the British Chemical Damp Course Association and the British Wood Preserving Association for the names and addresses of appropriate companies. The major companies will undertake a full survey and give a report on the property free of charge. If no problems are found they will offer insurance against timber problems in particular. If there are problems they will quote for them to be put right. Such a quote will be useful in price negotiation. The insurance schemes, while expensive, are a strong selling point in older property. A damp proof guarantee from a reputable company is a similarly valuable document.

If you are in doubt about any aspect of the property or if you are considering buying an older property, a structural survey is advisable. Such a survey will identify all the features of the property and locate any problems. The results of a structural survey will be useful for price negotiation as they will be an independent assessment of the property.

Structural surveys

Information about local qualified surveyors who undertake such work can be obtained from the Royal Institution of Chartered Surveyors. RICS also produce a number of useful leaflets for the potential house or flat purchaser.

Remember that you are instructing a surveyor, not vice versa, so it is important to discuss the extent of the survey and the fee at the outset. As there are no fixed charges for surveys, get more than one quotation. There are often significant variations. Travelling costs are included in the fee you pay, as is the cost of writing up the report. The report may be a useful tool in later negotiations with the vendor.

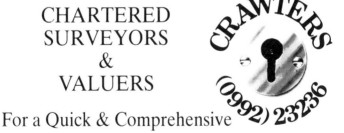

The cost of the survey, although not fixed, will be related in part to the purchase price of the property because that gives some indication of the liability the surveyor will bear if anything subsequently goes wrong which he has not identified. The surveyor carries appropriate insurance for this rare eventuality.

The cost, in 1988, for full structural surveys on two detached properties, one 22 years old, the other 80 years old, both valued at approximately £85,000, was £250 for the former and £425 for the latter. The differential reflects both the complexity of the work involved and the associated risk in two very different properties.

If you are negotiating a mortgage with a building society or other lender, you can ask them for a full structural survey at the same time as a valuation survey. Mortgages are dealt with in Chapter 5.

The survey can only include items which are reasonably visible.

Close inspection of the roof, for example, will be impossible and unless you make a specific request will be no more detailed than you could make yourself. The key difference is in the experience of the surveyor who will recognise the tell-tale signs of problems. The surveyor will look in roof spaces if there is reasonable access. Similarly, he will look at the underfloor structures, but only if there are suitable trap doors. In an occupied property, however, this may prove impossible because of floor coverings.

If you are buying a flat or maisonette it is equally relevant to have a survey undertaken, particularly in older property. In the case of a flat it is additionally important to assess the condition of the building as well as the flat itself, as you may be liable to repair and upkeep costs of the entire building. Consult the lease to identify your liabilities and make the surveyor aware of them too. As the overall property is the responsibility of all occupants you may find someone with a recent survey which you could look at or even pay to see.

If you are buying property on a new development, an individual survey may be unnecessary, since the company financing the project will have *their* surveyor regularly checking construction. They may co-operate with a building society who would accept the building specification as giving sufficient detail.

What to do with the survey
You will only have commissioned a survey if you are keen on the property. The survey will indicate any problems both major and minor in the property. It may indicate possible remedies. It is unlikely to advise on whether to purchase or not. It may indicate that the price should be lowered by an amount necessary to rectify the problems. You must decide yourself whether to purchase or not, and whether the price already allows for the work needed.

When making the decision, the extent of problems must be put in context. Three categories of problem are identifiable:

Minor cosmetic
These include decoration and general state of repair. While decoration and the kitchen units may not be to your taste or the paintwork is peeling, these are matters which can be disregarded. Most rooms in a house are redecorated every five years on average, so it will not be long before you would redecorate anyway. Similarly, kitchen units are replaced far more often than is really necessary: every six or seven years on average. The cost of this work is consequently absorbed in ongoing general maintenance.

Minor structural
Many minor structural problems can be undertaken by the competent DIY person. Such work may include replacing central heating boilers and radiators, replacing rotten doors and even windows, and repairs to guttering and down pipes. DIY is becoming increasingly popular and easy as the retail DIY stores are catering for the more sophisticated DIY person. In these instances the cost of work will not necessarily be onerous.

Major structural
This type of work is the job for experts and should be carefully assessed and costed before the purchase is progressed further. Settling of foundations, major damp, rotten timbers and roof defects are problems which are expensive to rectify. The cost of a new roof can be a crippling expense on top of an already large mortgage.

Buying older property

For many people the problems discussed above are perfectly acceptable because they deliberately buy older property with a view to 'doing it up'. The major advantage of this approach to buying a house or flat is that the capital costs can be kept to a minimum as the property will be cheaper and the renovation work can be done out of revenue over time. This is particularly important for first-time buyers with limited funds.

The major drawback of such an approach is that even with professionals doing the work it can take years to complete. For the DIY person it can become a life-time commitment.

Grants and assistance

It may be more difficult to borrow money to purchase a house in need of considerable repair. Some lenders may require a plan of the renovation work before being convinced.

Grants are available from the local authority for improvements, although there are certain conditions attached: for example, the house must be freehold and not a second home. The Department of the Environment publishes a useful booklet *Home Improvement Grants: a Guide to Home Owners, Landlords and Tenants.* Similar booklets are available in Scotland and Northern Ireland.

Two grants are available.

- *Intermediate grant.* Available for the installation for the first time of basic amenities, bath, hot and cold water and flush toilet, plus associated work. This grant is generally mandatory and is calculated as a percentage of eligible work.
- *Improvement grant.* This grant is discretionary and is intended to uprate existing property.

Go into your local authority housing or technical services department to enquire about grants. The availability of grants will vary from one authority to another and may depend on the number of applications received in any one period. Funds are limited in each financial year. On the other hand, discretionary grants are frequently made more readily towards the end of the financial year when budgets are underspent.

For older property which is of architectural significance (referred to as a 'listed building'), additional grants are available both from the local authority and from English Heritage.

Converting older buildings to flats
On a more ambitious scale you may consider buying a larger building with a view to conversion into flats, retaining one of the flats for personal occupation. For the individual with a little entrepreneurial flair this can be a very successful way of providing accommodation with profits. Larger Victorian houses in particular provide an ideal starting point for a flat conversion. The organisation SAVE has recently published a book illustrating the possibilities for using churches for conversion purposes: *Churches: A Question of Conversion,* by Ken Powell and Celia de la Hey.

Planning permission may become an issue if you purchase 'unusual' property for conversion. Redundant churches, barns, schools and warehouses will all require 'change of use' permission from the local planning authority. In the case of barns, many authorities are reluctant to allow the change to a non-agricultural use.

Can I afford to buy?

Whether you can or cannot afford to buy the property is clearly the crucial issue in the final decision. For this reason it has been left to this stage. However, the financial decision requires two questions to be answered:

1. Can I afford to move house?
2. Can I afford to buy this particular house or flat?

1. The first decision will involve three separate questions:
    (a) Can I afford to take on or increase the mortgage commitment?
    (b) Can I afford the expense of moving itself?
    (c) Can I afford the costs involved in living at a different location?
(a) Whether to take on the mortgage commitment will be based on an assessment of current income and expenditure and realistic expectations of change in both. Over the

last few years, in spite of recession, many people have found that their disposable income has risen well above the rates of inflation, leaving them surpluses which could be spent on housing. Because of tax relief on mortgage interest repayments and the desire to maximise that gain, the dubious notion of being under-mortgaged has arisen. This notion suggests that if a building society will lend two and a half times one's salary, for example, in order to maximise tax advantage and possibly longer-term capital appreciation, one should seek to maintain the 2.5 times relationship between mortgage and income as income rises. This, of course, assumes that one has no interests in life other than property, capital accumulation and mini-mising tax obligations!

(b) The expenses of moving can be very high and, because they involve a range of cost factors, are only in part related to the distance of the move. If you are moving because of job relocation, some or all of the expense may be covered by your employer. Most public and private sector employers give movement packages, although their generosity can vary significantly. If you are moving to a new job the position is slightly different. Many local authorities, for example, make no contribution towards the relocation expenses of their professional staff. There are now major regional variations in relocation packages because of the difficulty in attracting staff.

The major costs of buying and selling property and the associated costs of the move will include:

sale fees including estate agent's fee, advertising costs etc;
survey fees;
legal costs;
associated legal costs such as Land Registry fees, stamp duty, search fees;
removal and storage charges;
incidental expenses such as overnight accommodation and travelling expenses, connection and reconnection charges and mail redirection;
possible bridging loan charges.

It is quite easy to make approximations of each of these costs by obtaining quotations from the various people involved. As many of the costs are related to the price of the property, and the distance involved in the case of removal firms, an approximation is easily calculated. Add on a 20 per cent contingency to allow for errors or omissions. (Stamp duty is a tax levied at the rate of 1 per cent on the value of property over £30,000, ie on a property costing £20,000 no duty is payable. On a property costing £75,000 the stamp duty will be £750.)

Do the calculations for your own personal circumstances to assess whether, with all other outgoings, there is money available for a mortgage or increased mortgage. While much discussion is devoted to 'what you can borrow', it is important to assess for yourself what you can afford to pay.

(c) The costs of living at a new house or flat will clearly vary depending on the location and type of property you buy. However, there are general issues which should be considered:

Location – a change of location may influence day-to-day travel costs to work, to shop and to school. The change may necessitate the purchase of a car (first or second).

Size of property will influence:

insurance costs;

maintenance costs;

heating costs;

rateable value and rates payable (the rating system in England and Wales is currently in the process of major change. It is proposed to introduce a community charge or poll tax and abolish the rating system. Similar changes have already been introduced in Scotland.)

In a flat:

Service charges and sinking funds.

At the end of this analysis of costs you will decide whether or not you can afford to buy and whether the type of property you would like to purchase is within your grasp at this stage, and before you begin to look at specific properties it is advisable to establish in principle whether you can borrow the amount of money that you need.

2. When you have found a property that you like and wish to

purchase comes the second question, can I afford this particular property? At this stage you will be able to cost in detail many of the factors which were noted above including precise figures for the cost of the mortgage etc. You can also add in specific costs relating to the building itself, such as:

repairs to the structure (roof, damp course, rewiring, replacement of heating system, repair of fences);
modifications required (installation of heating system, building a garage);
cost of carpets and curtains.

Although some of these costs may be included in the new mortgage, they need to be identified and assessed.

One final cost should be added to your list at this point. That of your time, and the stress likely to arise during the process of buying, moving and settling into a new house or flat.

If you are confident that you can finance all these costs it is time to put in an offer for the property and the machinery of house or flat purchase will begin to grind away.

Chapter 4

The Formalities of Buying

Having decided that the property suits your requirements and that in principle you can afford to buy, you now begin the process of trying to purchase. The word 'try' is used advisedly as you may feel from time to time a lack of enthusiasm, particularly on the part of the professionals, to facilitate the sale. Do not despair. Professionals are involved in the process day in, day out and have their own procedures for dealing with things. Unlike you they are not emotionally involved and may at times appear uninterested.

The entire process is best seen as a series of stages as indicated in the following sections. The process is different in Scotland. The main elements of the Scottish approach are outlined at the end of this chapter.

1. Make an offer

Making an offer for the property does little more than establish the fact that you are interested in purchasing. The offer can be made through the vendor or his agent. Before making an offer it is useful to establish what the current market position of the property is. For example:

- Are any other offers outstanding on the property?
- If so, how many firm offers have been received?
- How long have the offers been in effect?

If there are other offers outstanding at the price you are willing to pay or if you cannot obtain answers to these questions, think seriously about proceeding. It is not uncommon for an additional offer to be used as a lever to hurry along another purchaser.

Any offer you make will be 'subject to contract'. This ensures that you are not liable for any of the vendor's costs if you subsequently decide not to purchase. Do not make offers for property you have little intention of buying. At this stage, the only reasons which should prevent your finally purchasing the property include:

- an unsatisfactory survey report;
- your inability to raise finance on the specific property;
- the searches or other investigations show problems with the property which have a major bearing on its suitability (road widening, plans for new factories on an adjacent site).

What price do I offer?
The asking price for the property will be based on a sale valuation either by an estate agent or by the vendor with reference to prevailing local prices. As suggested in Chapter 1, the sale valuation will reflect both the character of the property and what the agent thinks he can get for it. Do bear in mind that agents are paid a commission of 1 to 2 per cent of the sale price on completion of the sale. There is frequently some variation between agents' valuations, dependent on their perceptions of the market and their own business.

Additionally, most vendors are anxious to obtain the highest price possible for their property. Vendors tend to use the agent who gives the highest valuation.

Deciding on what price to offer involves your making judgements about all these factors. Most important, it depends on your awareness of the local market. If you have been looking for property for several months you will have gained a feel for how properties are selling and how prices are moving. Broad current trends were noted in Chapter 1. There will, though, be variations on individual property types. Establish how long the property has been on the market and how many other parties have made offers. Ultimately the offer must reflect how much you can afford to pay and your interest in not losing it to a higher bidder.

The market is very different in the various regions of the country. In the South East, pressures necessitate that you act quickly. In some other regions you can adopt the wait and see

approach once you have made your offer. If you are buying in a sellers' market then you may be faced with having to persuade the vendor to sell to you. In this case there are one or two good bargaining points worth emphasising.

- If you are a first-time buyer you will not have the problems of selling your own property. No chains of sellers and buyers will be involved and the purchase will be relatively straightforward.
- If you have already sold your own house you can similarly exchange contracts quickly.
- Establish in principle that you can borrow the necessary money for the purchase. Obtain a mortgage certificate to this effect to convince the vendor.
- You are interested in buying all the fixtures and fittings which are offered for sale separately.

You may be asked to place a deposit as a token of your intentions. The vendor or his agent will also ask for the name and address of your solicitor or conveyancer. The deposit is subject to contract and survey and you should obtain a receipt to that effect. The deposit does not bind either party and is returnable if for any reason contracts are not exchanged.

2. Notify your agents and advisers

- Notify your solicitor or conveyancer that you have made an offer for the property so that they can anticipate events. They will need to know the name of the vendor, the address of the property, and the names and addresses of the vendor's solicitor and estate agent.
- Inform the bank or building society from which you intend to borrow the money to purchase. Fill in the appropriate mortgage application forms and ask the bank or building society to undertake a valuation survey.

The society or bank will make a charge for this survey and usually will request the fee before the survey is undertaken. Some societies and banks insist that you pay the valuer directly. An indication of valuation fees is given on page 56 As you can see the fee depends on the estimated property value.

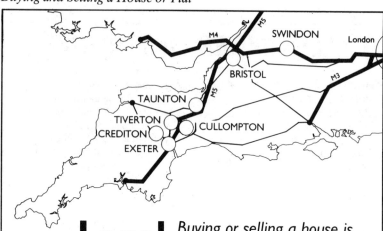

Estimated property value (£)	Indicative fee (£)
20,000	64.00
30,000	73.00
40,000	78.00
50,000	82.00
100,000	106.00

The fee is payable for each property you wish to consider for mortgage purposes. If you lose the property you lose the fee. Ask the vendor to let you know if he receives and accepts other offers as quickly as possible as you may be able to stop the valuation survey and save yourself money.

It is important to be clear about exactly what a mortgage valuation survey is. It is not a structural survey although it may note structural deficiencies. Its basic purpose is to establish the market value of the property to ensure that in the event of payment default for any reason, the building society could repossess the property and sell it at a high enough price to recover its loan. If the valuer assesses a value below the asking price, that will be the base figure from which the bank or building society will calculate the advance.

The joint RICS/ISVA publication, *Mortgage Valuations Explained*, notes that valuations take into account the following characteristics of a property:

- age, type, accommodation, fixtures and features;
- construction and general state of repair;
- siting and general amenities of the area;
- tenure, tenancies, annual payments and liabilities.

The valuation will disregard any planning potential of the property and associated gain and any inducements offered as part of the sale. If the assessed value is substantially lower than the asking price, it may be possible to negotiate a reduction with the vendor.

It is now usual for the bank or building society to let you see a copy of the valuation report. Increasingly the financial institutions are encouraging the joint use of surveyors and valuers to minimise costs. As a consequence it is possible to have a structural survey and valuation survey undertaken at the same time, reducing overall costs. However, in a dynamic market it is wise to give careful consideration to the expense of

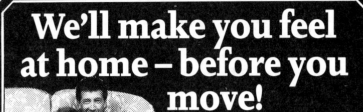

a structural survey until you are quite sure that the vendor is committed to your offer.

Valuation surveys may recommend one of three courses of action to the lender.

- The asking price reflects the market value and a loan can be made against the security of the property.
- The asking price reflects the market value of the property if certain repairs or treatments are undertaken. In these circumstances the lender might either:
  - make the advance with the proviso that the required work is completed within a given time; or
  - withhold part of the advance until the required work has been completed satisfactorily.
- The property is not reasonable security for a loan to be granted.

In the latter case it may be worthwhile to seek a second opinion or approach another society. Generally, the recommended course of action is to look for another property.

If the valuation survey or your own assessment suggests that there may be problems with the property, now is the time to consider whether to commission a professional survey (see Chapter 3). In either case, use the information revealed in the surveys to renegotiate the agreed price. Remember that your offer was made subject to contract and survey so that it is quite reasonable to suggest a lower price which better reflects the state of the property. These negotiations should have one of two objectives:

- to lower the agreed price in line with estimates of the cost of remedial work; or
- to ensure that remedial work is undertaken by the vendor prior to completion.

Some level of compromise is best accepted in these instances. If the vendor is unwilling to accept either proposition, depending on your interest in the property, it may be advisable to look for another house.

3. Put your own property on the market

If you have not already done so before starting your house search you should now put your own house on the market (see Chapter 8).

4. The interim period

This period is the most nerve-racking of the house purchase process. It is a period of wait and see during which you have virtually no control. The time can be well spent planning the move itself.

As there is no binding agreement during the period up to the exchange of contracts it is possible to lose the property altogether to a higher bidder or someone who can complete more quickly. It is wise to keep in frequent contact with the vendor and his agent so as to be fully aware of changes in terms.

While most agents would advise to the contrary, it is often found that a vendor has instructed two, three or even four contracts to be issued to competing purchasers. The first to undertake the necessary formalities gets the property. While benefiting the vendor this is not a practice to be recommended. Ask your solicitor to establish whether this is the case or not. Such contract races can prove expensive for those who do not win and you may be well advised to pull out of the race.

The agent is obliged to inform the vendor of any offers received up to the exchange of contracts. The agent can be held liable for negligence if he fails to so do. This means that the vendor may break his agreement with you and accept a higher offer. This activity, which came to the fore in the early 1970s when demand for houses was very high, is referred to as 'gazumping'. The practice has become common again as more and more people chase a limited stock of houses.

If you are gazumped you will usually be given the chance to better the offer. It is often difficult to know what course to take as to offer more might simply start an inflationary price spiral. You will have to weigh up the costs you have already incurred, which of course will be wasted, against the increased mortgage payments. The problem may be simply resolved because you cannot borrow enough money. Gazumping frequently takes the price of the property well above any mortgage valuation.

Solicitors are well aware of the difficulties associated with the practice of gazumping. The Law Commission's Conveyancing Standing Committee has devised a system of pre-contract deposits which would allow for compensation to the purchaser and loss of deposit to the vendor if a higher offer from another

vendor is accepted. Details of this system are available from the Law Commission.

Never give up hope until you see the new occupiers actually move in. Many things can go wrong in house purchase and the sale may fall through. It is advisable to keep in touch with the vendor or agent to the end. A chain might break down, the purchaser may be unable to finance the purchase. It is not uncommon for an agent to contact you six or eight weeks after a sale was agreed to enquire if you are still interested.

5. The legal process

The legal process involved in purchasing a house or flat is referred to as conveyancing. This is simply the conveying of the ownership of the property from one person to another. The actual process itself is straightforward if longwinded. However, problems do arise during the conveyancing process which can slow it up and cause undue complication. In England and Wales there are three ways of conveyancing the property:

- appoint your own solicitor;
- appoint a licensed conveyancer;
- do the conveyancing yourself.

These three possibilities have arisen only in recent years since the solicitors' monopoly has been broken. The DIY method is growing slowly in popularity. Assuming that you take a systematic logical approach to the process and use one of the DIY conveyancing manuals you should have few problems. Doing the work yourself has some advantages.

- You control the pace of the process.
- You save yourself money.
- You remain in control.

However, there are several disadvantages which should make you think twice before you act. The major disadvantages are these.

- You will be emotionally involved and hence may have difficulty keeping to a strict programme of events.

- If difficulties occur you may have to take legal advice for which you will have to pay.
- If you are in receipt of a mortgage the building society will insist on a solicitor being employed for some of the work.

There are certain circumstances where you are strongly advised not to do the work yourself. These include:

- a property which is not registered;
- a property which is being bought new from a builder;
- property other than houses;
- property outside England and Wales.

Solicitors or conveyancers

Choosing between a solicitor and a conveyancer is really a matter of personal choice. Both will undertake the legal transfer of the property for you and both will charge you a fee. If you already use a solicitor for other work then it is probable that you will instruct this practice to deal with your house or flat. If it is a small general solicitors' practice with little specialist work in property you may consider turning elsewhere.

The best way of finding a solicitor is by recommendation, of friends or colleagues, or by bank manager, building society or estate agent. Lists of solicitors are found in the Law Society's *Regional Directory* or you can simply consult Yellow Pages or the local paper.

Lists of licensed conveyancers can be obtained from either the Council for Licensed Conveyancers, or the Association of Licensed Conveyancers. Before making a final decision ask for quotations for the work to be done. As in other activities it is wise to get three or more estimates. Up to 1973 the solicitor's charge was on a scale depending on the cost of the property. Now the charge relates much more closely to the actual work done, the complexity of the transaction and the value of the property. Quotations are often negotiable as solicitors are in a competitive market. There will be some fixed elements in the fee for payments the solicitor makes on your behalf to other agencies. These will include stamp duty, fees to the local council for searches and to the Land Registry if the property has to be registered. These fees can be calculated at the outset to give you an idea of total costs.

What will the solicitor do?

Your solicitor will undertake several tasks as part of the conveyancing process. There are three main elements of these tasks.

- Checking that the property is as described, is for sale by the vendor and has no technical difficulties associated with it. He will obtain the deeds to the property to check them and decide whether any additional clauses need to be added as a result of subsequent modification. He will check with the planning authority if necessary to establish whether the property has planning permission and will check with the vendor's solicitor if the appropriate permissions were obtained for any extensions or modifications since the property last changed hands. He will also check with the local authority that no new development, such as road widening, is likely to affect the property. All these enquiries come under the general term 'searches'. (These searches can take a considerable time to complete. There has been severe criticism of several local authorities for taking as long as three months.)
- Drawing up a contract of sale. The vendor's solicitor will draw up a draft contract of sale during this period in anticipation of there being no major snags arising from the searches. The draft contract will specify the detailed conditions of the sale. As your solicitor or conveyancer is unlikely to visit the property and will base his work on information provided to him, it is crucial that you raise all the issues which you think are important. Your solicitor will also send a standard set of questions, the 'preliminary enquiries', to the vendor's solicitor.

  The draft contract frequently goes back and forth between solicitors until it is in an agreed format for the final contract. This part of the transaction can take some time and anything up to 10 weeks can be regarded as normal. Causes of delays vary between purchasers and properties but include:
  - problems on the part of the vendor which are slowing down his purchase. He may himself be in a chain or be having problems with his own purchase;
  - the local authority searches may be taking a long time;

- difficulties in verifying information about the property you are purchasing;
- delays in obtaining a mortgage offer from your building society.

• The third element of the solicitor's work is the exchange of contracts. This is an important step because it marks the time at which you enter into a contract with associated liabilities with the vendor and vice versa. To withdraw from the sale contract for any reason after the exchange of contracts will cost either party money. Normally the solicitor will ask you to visit his office to sign the contract. At this time he will discuss in detail all aspects of the contract. If you are uncertain about anything, do ask. It is not necessary for you to visit the office if this is inconvenient. The matter can be dealt with by post quite easily.

The following particular points are worth considering in detail when the solicitor discusses with you the terms of the draft contract.

— Be quite sure what of the house contents you are buying and what the vendors are taking with them. Frequently the solicitor or conveyancer will indicate 'see agents particulars' in the contract. The sale will then include all the items on the original description. However, the list will not be exhaustive: it will not mention light bulbs and fittings or telephones, for example. It is advisable to draw up a list as indicated in Appendix 4. This will prevent any misunderstanding and upset when you actually move into the house. If the vendors take additional items with them they will be in breach of contract and your solicitor will be able to help you recover the loss. Such items will, of course, exclude those which you are purchasing outside the formal house sale.
— Take particular care with the definition of the boundary. Many arguments between neighbours arise through boundary disputes. Check with the deeds exactly where the boundary lies: do not rely on the line of a fence or trees. Also check who owns which fences and whether there are any restrictions over fences and fence heights.

You are unlikely to be asked to sign and exchange contracts until all the checking is complete. The solicitor is liable for any errors caused. Normally all the searches, the preliminary enquiries, confirmation of mortgage, deposit and agreed completion date will have been received by this time.

It is at this point that you will pay the vendor 10 per cent of the purchase price as a deposit.

In the period, say two weeks, before the expected exchange, make arrangements to have the deposit ready, or if going for a 100 per cent mortgage, make sure that the mortgage advance of deposit is available for exchange of contracts, ie a bridging loan.

The final role the solicitor plays is arranging for the completion of the sale. Quite simply, this is the stage at which your solicitor hands over the balance of the money for the property and the vendor's solicitor gives your solicitor the legal document which transfers the 'title' to the land to you. In practice the process is usually slightly more involved.

The formalities of buying in Scotland

There are both similarities and differences in the buying of property between Scotland and the rest of the United Kingdom. This section concentrates on the main differences and should be read in conjunction with what has already been said about the general process.

Sources of information

In addition to the press the main sources of information about property in Scotland are:

- *Solicitors.* Solicitors sell the vast majority of properties in Scotland. In many areas solicitors have set up 'property centres' which provide information about property. Some produce regular lists of property they are selling. A list of the property centres can be obtained from the Law Society of Scotland. Some solicitors have their own property departments.
- *Estate agents.* Estate agencies are increasing in Scotland, having been virtually unknown until the mid-1960s. They operate in a similar way to those in the rest of the UK.

Procedure

Almost all property is bought and sold with the help of a solicitor. The Law Society of Scotland will provide you with names and addresses if necessary. There is no scale of fees for the work involved so it is essential to shop around for estimates. If the property is over £30,000 you will have to pay stamp duty of 1 per cent of the price. There will also be registration charges for the Register of Sasines or Land Register of Scotland.

It is normal to be advised by your solicitor on the price to offer when you have found a suitable property. It may be that several offers have been received for the property. There will be a closing date on which all offers will be considered.

Any surveys on the property are undertaken before an offer is made. This is the one major disadvantage of the Scottish system because you may lose the property to a higher bidder after going to the expense of a survey. Once the offer is accepted, a binding agreement is made for your purchase of the property. Unlike the position in England, acceptance of the offer gives you certain possession. Once the offer is accepted the two solicitors will exchange 'missives', the legally binding contract.

The purchase is completed by delivery of the title deeds and disposition in exchange for the payment cheque. This can be as soon as a few days after the exchange of missives.

Chapter 5

Financing Your Purchase

Reference was made in Chapter 3 to finance for house purchase. In this chapter the major issues of property finance are outlined in some detail along with the considerations you should take into account when arranging finance for the purchase.

Mortgages

The loan for property purchase is referred to as a mortgage. In principle it is exactly the same as a normal loan except that it is usually given for a longer period, between 10 and 25 years. The interest paid to the lender is variable through time. Your property is used as security for the loan so that in the event of default on payments, the property can be sold and the loan repaid. In this way the lender is unlikely to lose.

Until recently the major sources of mortgages for house purchase were the building societies. Recently the market has widened and a number of other sources are now available.

Building societies

The building societies still lend the major amount of money for house purchase. The society movement is made up of the large societies such as the Halifax, Abbey National, Anglia Nationwide, National and Provincial and the Leeds Permanent and a large number of smaller societies. Most are members of the Building Societies Association which until recently regulated the pattern of trading of the individual societies. Now each society is able to act as it wishes, hence a degree of variation and competition is developing in the mortgage market.

Most of the larger societies are organised on a regional and

local branch basis. The branch manager has a loans budget and
discretion on the loans he grants. Availability of mortgages
varies considerably depending on the amounts of money being
invested in the societies and other external financial factors.
Some societies give preference to existing customers, both
lenders and borrowers. Particularly if you are buying your first
house you should consider opening an account with one or
more societies well in advance of needing a mortgage.

Do shop around. There is considerable competition developing between the societies which has led to increasing
variation in the terms offered.

In many areas both solicitors and estate agents act as agents
for building societies and have allocations of funds for loan.
Your estate agent or solicitor may be able to help you with
raising adequate finance.

Banks
Over the last few years the banks have become increasingly
involved in the mortgage business because it offers them
particularly attractive and secure rates of return. All the major
high street banks offer mortgage facilities. Many of the less
familiar foreign banks are also in the market. In general the
banks tend to lend larger amounts than the building societies.
This is particularly the case with foreign banks who are increasingly active in London and the South East where large
loans are required.

Insurance companies
Several insurance companies offer mortgages. These are
usually linked to endowment life assurance.

Local authorities
If you are buying your property under the 'right to buy'
scheme you should be able to obtain a mortgage from the local
authority. However, the availability of such mortgages varies
significantly. Many local authorities restrict the number each
year and consequently you need to apply early in the financial
year.

Builders
If you are buying a new house you may be offered a mortgage

0 to 100% in just 30 minutes

Pick up the phone, dial 01-255 2581 right now and in minutes we'll tell you whether you can get the mortgage you want.

If you decide to proceed, you may be a little surprised at just how quickly we get things done from start to finish.

As independent advisors, we don't just offer you a fast streamlined service. We also strive to find the best possible mortgage to suit your needs.

These are some of the ways in which we can help:

- 100% mortgages up to £120,000.
- Maximum income multipliers.
- Remortgages (We could reduce your interest payments up to 35% in the first year.)
- Non-status mortgages.
- Repayment, endowment and pension mortgages to suit your needs.
- Special low start mortgages.

Call Paul Lambert on 01-255 2581.

CMG Carlton Retirement Planning Ltd. Mappin House Winsley Street London W1

CMG is a service offered by Carlton Retirement Planning Limited, a Fimbra member.

Consumer Credit Licence No: 148291.

by the builder. Many of the larger building companies now offer low cost starter mortgages or 100 per cent mortgages particularly intended for first-time buyers. These deals are very attractive inducements to buy. Do remember that the builder will recoup the costs of such schemes in other ways, such as higher house prices.

Employers

Many employers now offer mortgage facilities to their staff as a fringe benefit. This is particularly true of the banks, insurance companies and building societies where preferential, discounted interest rates are frequently available. Before you enter into such a scheme check the terms of the offer very carefully. What happens to the loan if you leave the company? Does it have to be repaid or is the interest rate increased to the normal commercial level?

Mortgage brokers

Strictly speaking, mortgage brokers do not lend money, but arrange loans with other parties such as banks, insurance companies and building societies. Normally there is little to be gained from using a broker unless you are buying an unusual property or need a particularly large loan. In these circumstances a broker may be able to arrange suitable finance. Usually there will be a fee to pay.

Many brokers specialise in endowment-linked loans (see page 86). In these cases no fee is charged as the insurance company will pay the broker a commission for gaining the business.

Private loans

It may be possible range a private loan from a relative or friend. Although such loans are not common, one may solve a particular mortgage problem by being offered at a low rate of interest or with deferred repayments. If you are fortunate to obtain a private loan do ensure that a proper contract is drawn up between yourself and the lender. Tax relief can be claimed on the interest you pay on a loan up to £30,000. The lender will have to declare the interest you pay to the Inland Revenue.

81

Different types of mortgage

There are four main categories of mortgage: the repayment mortgage, the endowment mortgage, the pension mortgage and the unit-linked mortgage. Each of these types works in a different way and offers advantages and disadvantages to the borrower, usually depending on income, tax position and employment.

Repayment mortgage

Repayments are made monthly for the length of the loan. The amount you will pay each month will depend on the amount borrowed, the length of the loan and the interest rate at the time. Each payment is made up of two parts: part repayment of the capital, and interest on the capital outstanding. As the loan progresses, the relative importance of capital and interest changes. At the outset of a loan, most of the payment is interest, but as the capital is slowly paid back, the interest component decreases to become only a small element at the end of the period.

Normally, the changes in 'mix' of capital and interest are averaged out over the period of the mortgage for tax purposes. Consequently, you pay a constant amount throughout the loan. This is usually referred to as a 'level repayment' mortgage. You may, however, consider an 'increasing payment' mortgage more appropriate. In this case the tax relief available on interest is not averaged out over the period of the loan. Consequently, maximum tax relief is achieved at the beginning of the loan. This has the effect of increasing the repayments of the mortgage over time as the mix of interest to capital changes. This type of repayment is particularly useful for the first-time buyer as it reduces the repayment at the beginning of the mortgage which is usually the time when it can be afforded least! Some building societies are favouring this approach at present because it eases the repayments particularly for first-time buyers.

Some societies offer special low cost starter mortgages with reduced payments in the first few years.

An indication of the cost of a mortgage is given opposite. The actual example will vary as interest rates and tax levels change.

Both examples illustrate the way in which the increasing repayment method affects the actual amount you pay for your mortgage at the beginning and end of its term.

83

Example 1. A repayment mortgage over 25 years for £24,000 at an interest rate of 11.25 per cent assuming the increasing repayment method.

Total monthly payment	£241.83
Total payment less tax (in first year)	£181.08
Total payment less tax (final year)	£235.22

If the term of the mortgage is extended to 30 years the payment would work out as in Example 2.

Example 2. A repayment mortgage over 30 years for £24,000 at an interest rate of 11.25 per cent assuming the increasing repayment method.

Total monthly payment	£234.58
Total payment less tax (in first year)	£173.83
Total payment less tax (final year)	£228.17

If for one reason or another you cannot afford the repayments during the life of a repayment mortgage two alternatives are usually open to you. First, you can extend the length of the mortgage. As you can see in the example above, this does not have a major impact on repayments. Alternatively, the lender may agree to defer capital payments so that you only pay the interest charges. As explained above, the effect that this will have will depend on when during the life of the loan the problem arises.

If you become unemployed or for other reasons have to claim income support, you may be entitled to help with mortgage interest. Normally interest payments are added to your personal allowance. Unless you or your partner are over 60, only half the interest will be paid in the first 16 weeks. In these circumstances consult your Citizens' Advice Bureau to get help with your case before going to the Social Security Office.

85

If you move house before the term of the mortgage is completed, the proceeds of the sale are used to pay off the balance owing. A new mortgage is then obtained on the property you wish to purchase in the normal way.

Endowment mortgage

An endowment mortgage is one which is linked to a life insurance policy. During the course of the mortgage you pay interest only to the bank or building society, the capital being paid at the end of the period in a lump sum by use of the endowment policy. In addition you take out an endowment policy to the value of the capital borrowed. When the policy matures, or if you die before that date, the mortgage is paid off.

The cost of the endowment policy will vary depending on the length of the policy, your age and health. Three types of endowment policy are generally available.

Non-profit endowment
The cover given is exactly the same as the capital borrowed.

With-profit endowment
In this case the policy is for the amount of the capital borrowed. In addition, however, you share in the profits of the company and a bonus is added to the sum assured each year. At the end of the term the policy will both pay the capital borrowed and provide you with a surplus. The surplus will depend on the performance of the company. Because you are sharing in the profit of the company, this type of policy will cost significantly more than a non-profit policy.

Low-cost endowment
This type of policy has grown in popularity in recent years. It is really a combination of the two other types. Cover is taken to cover the capital in two parts:

- *With profits for half the policy.* It is assumed that the profits made over the term of the mortgage will be enough to cover the whole amount of capital borrowed.
- *Life cover for half the mortgage.* In the event of your death before the with-profits element matures, the life cover will ensure that the balance of the mortgage can be paid.

Low-cost endowment policies are much cheaper than full with-profits policies. However, because there is an element of risk, check with your building society or bank that the company you are thinking of dealing with is acceptable.

If you cannot meet the repayments with an endowment mortgage you are faced with fewer alternatives than a repayment type. As you are only paying interest you cannot defer capital payment, nor can you extend the period of the loan. The only real alternative is to convert the policy to a repayment type and cash in the policy to help pay off the capital of the loan.

Pension mortgages

A pension mortgage is similar to an endowment mortgage in that only interest is paid during the life of the mortgage. The capital payment is made by linking the mortgage to one of the pension plans now offered by most insurance companies. On retirement, the lump sum provided by the plan pays off the capital outstanding.

Pension linked schemes are particularly tax efficient for

those on higher rates of tax, as tax relief is allowed on both the interest and the pension contributions. At present pension mortgages are only available to those who are self-employed or do not have an employer's pension scheme.

Pension plan mortgages are similar to endowment mortgages in the case of moving house. A major problem with pension plan mortgages, however, is their inflexibility. If you are unable to keep up the payments you will usually be obliged to repay the loan.

Unit-linked mortgage

Interest is paid as in the other 'linked' mortgages. Payment to the insurance company in this case is for direct investment. The value of the policy at the end of the term will depend directly on the performance of the investment. There is now a wide range of unit-linked policies to choose from, linked to unit trusts, property, building societies and fixed interest investments. These types of mortgage were becoming increasingly popular as the stock market prices rose over the last three years or so. As the value of the policy depends on the performance of the investment, many people are now very concerned about the value of their assets after the stock market crash. There is always this risk when you take out this type of mortgage.

The recent crash on the stock market has emphasised the risks involved in all types of mortgages that have a with-profits content. Fortunately, most of the major companies played down the growth in the market when making their forecasts and most are currently paying bonuses in line with previous years.

Which type of mortgage?

The type of mortgage you choose will depend on your personal circumstances and particularly your tax status. The only way to be absolutely sure what is best for you is to ask for repayment figures to be calculated for each type for your particular case. Only then can direct comparison be made on which to base your decision. Appendix 7 gives you an indication of the kind of calculations and comparisons you can expect to receive. In this particular example, the low-cost endowment is probably the best option.

In addition to the cost of the mortgage itself there may be additional charges associated with each of the different mortgages. These will include:

- the lender's valuation fee;
- the lender's solicitor's fee;
- your solicitor's fee (for handling the mortgage);
- an arrangement fee (bank mortgage);
- higher legal fees (endowment mortgage);
- mortgage protection policy (repayment mortgage).

How much can I borrow?

This question is best asked in reverse: How much can you afford to pay back? There are variations in terms between the different societies but there are some general rules which apply.

- *Maximum advances.* These vary with the property valuation. For example:

Price or valuation	Maximum advance	Maximum term
Up to £80,000	95%	25 years
£80,000 to £120,000	90% or minimum of £76,000	25 years
£120,000 to £160,000	85% or minimum of £108,000	25 years

Figures given above are general and will vary between individual properties and societies.

- *Income requirements.* These also vary between the various societies and it is worth shopping around to get the best deal. The following example gives you a general indication of what to expect:

Percentage advance	Over 75%	50–75%
One applicant	3× income	3.5 × income
Two applicants	3× higher + 1× lower or 2.5× joint incomes	3.5 × higher + 1 × lower or 2.75 × joint incomes

SCOTLAND'S LARGEST
INDEPENDENT MORTGAGE BROKERS

MORE THAN JUST
A MORTGAGE

We firmly believe that, just like a good suit, your mortgage should be tailored to fit your unique requirements.

This is why you will find within our extensive branch network a team of highly trained consultants who will sympathetically and professionally discuss and determine your needs.

Because no one in Scotland knows more about buying and selling a house, you will reap the benefit of our unrivalled guidance to successfully purchasing.

All of this without obligation or fee.

★ 100% Mortgages
★ Low Start/Low Cost Mortgages
★ Pension Mortgages
★ Registered Independent Financial Advisors
★ Branches throughout Scotland

For details of your nearest branch
Telephone: 041-638 8855

Branches at:

Airdrie, Ayr, Bridge of Weir, Burnside, Dumbarton, Dunfermline, East Kilbride, Falkirk, Glenrothes, Hamilton, Helensburgh, Kilmarnock, Kirkcaldy, Kirkintilloch, Largs, Paisley, Perth, Stirling, Troon.

Glasgow at Bearsden, Clarkston, Dennistoun, Mount Florida, Shawlands and West End.

Edinburgh at City Centre, Corstorphine and Penicuik.

FIMBRA
MEMBER

Licenced Credit Broker. Full written details on request.

These figures will give you a good idea of what you can borrow.

Unmarried couples are usually treated in the same way as married couples.

Multiple purchase, when more than two people buy a property together, it is more of a problem. Most building societies will not lend to more than two people because of the risks of the group splitting up. Some of the smaller societies and the insurance companies will grant loans, usually on a $1 + 1 + 1 \times 3$ basis, for three people. You may have to use a broker, however, to find these deals. Do remember that each member of the group is ultimately responsible for the total outstanding balance.

The rise in house prices in London and the South East has led some lenders to develop innovative approaches to home loans for certain groups. A scheme to provide nurses and other National Health Service workers in London with mortgages was recently launched by the Anglia Nationwide Society. The

scheme provides 100 per cent mortgages at two-thirds the usual interest rate. In return the Society will keep up to half the profits when a home is resold. This scheme reduces monthly payments on a £60,000 loan from £496 to £297 after tax.

When calculating the loan, lenders take into account your basic salary before deductions of tax etc. Some will take additional income such as overtime into account, although they will probably need written confirmation from your employer about the regularity of overtime. For those on salary scales which increase incrementally each year, some societies take these increments into account.

If you are self-employed, the lender will be interested in your accounts over a three- or four-year period. They will contact your accountant to verify the figures.

Tax and tax relief

Tax relief is given on mortgage interest at the highest rate of tax you pay. For people paying tax at 25 per cent this means that a 12 per cent interest rate actually costs you 8 per cent. Relief is given on mortgages of up to £30,000. Above that figure you pay the full interest rate. The tax relief is given at source under the MIRAS (Mortgage Interest Relief at Source) system so that the monthly payment you make already takes account of the tax relief. If you pay tax above the basic rate you will be allowed basic rate tax relief as normal and will have to negotiate with the Inland Revenue for tax relief on the higher rates.

Couples buying a house are allowed only £30,000 between them from 1 August 1988. However, anyone buying a house in joint or multiple purchase before that date will each be entitled to maximum tax relief.

House sale is free of capital gains tax. The concession applies only to one property designated by yourself as your main residence. If you own several properties you can decide which is to be the main residence; it does not have to be the one in which you spend most time. For tax purposes it is most advantageous for it to be the property from which you make most capital gain.

Finance and the first-time buyer

When you exchange contracts for your new house you will have to put down a deposit of between 5 and 10 per cent of the asking price. For first-time buyers there is a government scheme called Homeloan which is intended to help with the deposit and payments. There are two main benefits.

- A tax-free cash bonus of up to £110. This is payable if you have held £1,000 or more in a special building society account for 12 months.
- An additional loan of £600 interest free for the first five years of your mortgage.

There are conditions associated with this scheme which are explained in the Homeloan leaflet available from most building societies and banks.

Obtaining your mortgage

This process is best approached in three stages.

1. Deciding the type of loan you require and from which financial source.
2. Establishing in principle how much you can borrow and on what terms. The building societies realise the value of loans granted in principle prior to purchase negotiations. Some offer mortgage certificates which state how much they are prepared to lend, subject to a property valuation survey.
3. Negotiating the precise loan for a particular property.

It is advisable to undertake stages 1 and 2 before you begin to look for property, otherwise you may waste a lot of time for all concerned.

Normally the full application for the mortgage is specific to an individual property. However, with the introduction of the mortgage certificate, several societies will now ask you to complete two forms at different stages of the process.

There is no common mortgage application system and the questions asked will vary between societies. The Financial Services Act which came into force in April 1988 has forced many societies to modify their approach to mortgage applications and ask for more detailed personal financial information. Some societies insist on an interview with the potential client rather than the simple filling in of a form. Whichever approach is adopted by the society you choose you will be asked questions on the following issues:

- personal details;
- name;
- address;
- length of residence at that address;
- owner occupier or tenant;
- date of birth;
- marital status;
- any court judgments against you including credit transactions;
- details of bankers, solicitors etc;
- employment;
- name of employer and address;
- length of employment;
- previous employment;
- if self-employed, name and address of accountant;
- income in some detail including bonuses and overtime;
- outgoings;
- rent or mortgage;
- loans, including secured, business and unsecured loans, credit cards etc;
- details of current mortgage;
- address;
- current lender;
- amount borrowed, account number, amount outstanding;
- arrears;
- details of property being sold;
- details of property to be purchased;
- details of loan required:
  - type,
  - amount,
  - duration.

The mortgage, if granted, will be subject to conditions. Some of these conditions are of a general nature such as:

- keeping the property in a good state of repair;
- not taking in tenants without permission of the lender;
- seeking permission for any alterations to the property;
- insuring the property to the satisfaction of the lender.

Others will be specific to the property including undertaking specific repairs.

If you are not fortunate enough to get a mortgage first time, do not despair. It may be that funds are not currently available from the society you have approached. Alternatively, they may not be happy with the property itself.

It is often more difficult to obtain a large advance for:

- property of unconventional construction;
- leasehold property with only a few years remaining on the lease;
- flats or maisonettes above a certain number of floors (usually about four);
- flats above shops;
- properties which front directly on to the street;
- property built before a certain date;
- property with a sitting tenant;
- property without inside toilet and bathroom facilities;
- a converted flat rather than a purpose-built one.

In either case it is worth shopping around. If you currently have an investment with the society, make a fuss. Write to the regional manager and tell him that you will move your money elsewhere.

If the refusal is because of your personal circumstances, income, employment or age (ie, you are considered too young or too old to be a good risk), it may be worth reconsidering whether you should buy in the first place. Perhaps you cannot really afford the house.

There are still some prejudices in the house loan market towards certain groups of individuals and certain locations. For a long time building societies would not lend money on properties in certain inner city areas for example, the so-called 'red lining' policy. If you feel you may be the victim of such activity, go to the local Citizens' Advice Bureau.

Chapter 6
Completing the Purchase and Moving

In Chapter 4 the legal process of purchase was described. That process will end with the completion of the purchase. The solicitor or conveyancer will then send you his bill and hopefully all will have gone smoothly. There can be hiccups in the process, however, and it is better to anticipate them rather than ignore them.

Major problems are most likely to arise because of the chain effect of several houses being bought and sold at the same time. This becomes less likely the nearer you are to the first-time buyer situation, in which the person buying your property does not rely on others to purchase his or hers. Some chains in house purchase can be very long, six or more transactions being involved. In these situations the chances of things going wrong are quite high. It is possible to get around the chain problem in two ways.

- There are agencies who act as chain breakers in certain circumstances and buy the property involved, usually at substantial discount. Ask your agent or solicitor for information. If you are involved in a company move your company will be able to help.
- A bridging loan may be useful when you have to complete your purchase before your sale. It should only be used when you have exchanged contracts, and not to break chains. Normally a bank or building society will lend money when contracts are exchanged. Do take care, however, as bridging finance is expensive even though the interest paid is tax allowable.

    Some of the specialist agencies, such as Lloyds' Black Horse Agency, can arrange special open-ended bridging loans to break chains. It is wise to take advice before getting involved in such loans.

Once you have exchanged contracts and before the completion date there are several things which you need to consider in anticipation of the move.

Insurance

More will be said about insurance in Chapter 7. At this stage you should take out insurance cover on the new property. Once contracts have been exchanged the liability transfers to the purchaser. Some house structure policies provide automatic cover for this situation. Do check.

Rates

You will be responsible to the local authority for payment of rates once you have moved into your new house or flat. The liability formally begins when the purchase is completed but no charge is made until furniture is moved in. If there is a long period between completion and moving in, some authorities will levy a reduced rate on the unoccupied property. The rates levied are based on the rateable value and the 'poundage'.

- The rateable value of the property. This is decided by the Inland Revenue and is related to the size of the property and its amenities.
- The 'poundage'. This is the sum which the local authority levies per pound rateable value. If, for example, the rateable value is £100 and the poundage is £1.50, then the rates payable would be £150.

The rating system is currently undergoing major changes with the proposed introduction of a community charge or poll tax. In Scotland the process of change has already begun and the system will be replaced in 1992 by a tax levied on members of households over 18 years of age. A similar system is to be introduced in England and Wales.

It is important to contact the rating officer for your new area to obtain the information required to calculate the rates payable. You will only be responsible for rates for that part of the year in which you occupy the property. It is quite likely that you will receive a refund from the rating authority for your former house too. Usually this refund is made directly to you or, if you are moving within the same local authority area, it may be credited to your rating bill for the new property. In some circumstances your solicitor may simply debit the purchaser for the amount you have overpaid.

Water rates are collected separately in England and Wales and with the domestic rate in Scotland. In England and Wales it is important to inform the water authority of your impending move too so that any refunds can be made for your previous property and a new account be started for the new property.

Informing people of your move

It is important to inform people of your move. You will be surprised how long the list can be. Appendix 5 provides a list of possible people and groups to whom address change notification should be sent. Although the list is self-explanatory one or two comments may be useful.

Banks and building societies

In the case of banks and building societies it is not necessary to move your account to a nearer bank. As long as the bank has your new address almost all banking services can be carried out at another branch without transfer. It might be useful to establish an agreement for drawing out larger than normal amounts of money, to cover the changeover. If you intend to transfer the account this is best done well after the move so that you can check that it has been undertaken properly. While in theory moving an account is simply a matter of completing forms, it is complex in practice and can lead to delays in payments of standing orders etc. If you do not change your branch immediately it will save you the hassle of informing immediately all those who need to know the address of your bank, such as employer, credit card company, building society. The time to move accounts is three months after the move when all payments have been made and cleared and you are beginning to settle in.

Redirection of mail

The difficulties in ensuring that everyone who should be is informed of your move make it useful to have your mail redirected. It is possible for you to arrange with the purchaser of your property to forward any mail. If you are moving only a short distance you can arrange to call in periodically to pick it up. Do remember, though, that goodwill can soon break down if this task becomes onerous and extends over a long period. If you normally receive more than a couple of letters per day then you are strongly advised to use the mail forwarding service offered by the post office. This service will automatically redirect your mail to the new address; there is a charge for this, as follows:

Letters	*Up to one month*	*Additional three months*	*One year*
	£2.50	£5.75	£14.00

Parcels   A charge equivalent to the original postage is theoretically payable, but often is not charged.

Normally a week's notice is required to set the service in motion.

If you are staying at temporary accommodation between moves it may be useful to ask the post office to hold letters so that you can collect them personally.

Telephone

Telephones are another issue which can be sorted out in advance. You have more than one option, depending on the nature of your move. If you move within the existing telephone exchange area you can:

1. Retain your existing number   Cost £21
2. Take over the number at the
   new address   Cost £16
3. Have a new number on the
   existing line   Cost £21

If you are moving outside the present exchange area then options 2 and 3 will apply. If you are not taking your number with you it might be appropriate to consider having your calls redirected. The charge for this service is an initial fee of £22 and a further charge of £37 per quarter. There is a minimum period of one quarter for the service.

In all cases it is wise to give plenty of notice of your intentions. The redirection service will need a minimum of seven days' notice.

If the house or flat to which you are moving does not have a telephone already installed you will need to check whether there are British Telecom cables coming into the property and whether they are still serviceable. A BT engineer will readily come to advise you. If you require a new system this can be installed within eight working days. It will, however, cost £90. Incidentally, all BT charges are exclusive of VAT so do remember to add 15 per cent to the costs.

If you have your own plug-in phone units and do not rent units from BT you will be able to take them with you. Check that the house you are moving to has the appropriate sockets.

Full information on all your telephone needs can be obtained from BT Telephone Sales. Dial 100 and ask for Telephone Sales for the area you are moving to.

Many of the removal companies provide change of address and telephone cards free. British Telecom provide similar cards for changed telephone numbers. The earlier these are sent out the better.

Gas and electricity services
The gas and electricity boards will need to be informed of your departure from the old address and your move to the new one. Both services will come to read the meters on completion day and will need to be notified of the date in advance. It is also wise to check that the meters have been read at the new property. If you require assistance with the installation of appliances on completion day, the wiring up of an electric cooker, for example, give the relevant company plenty of warning.

In both cases you will have to fill in forms beforehand for the takeover of the supply.

If you will need any modification to the gas or electricity supply, now is the time to discuss your requirements. You may wish to use an alternative source for cooking or heating to that of the previous occupiers which will require fitting new sockets or pipework. In any older property in which, for example, gas has not been used for many years, the service pipe from the mains may no longer be safe and a new pipe will be needed.

While this is a straightforward and reasonably priced job, do not assume that it can be done the day you move in. If you are in doubt about any of the services, ask one of the respective engineers to discuss things with you well before the move. You may then be able to get work done when you require it. Always anticipate that work will take longer than you expect.

Curtains and carpets

If you intend to make up curtains yourself or modify your existing ones, visit the new property well in advance to measure up. Most vendors will be quite happy for carpet suppliers to measure up too. It is one indication to them that the sale is progressing and the end is in sight. Most sales exclude carpets and curtains and you will have established by now what is being left in your particular case. If the vendors suggest leaving old curtains and carpets that they no longer need and are not part of the sale, this may be a useful way of easing pressure on your first few days in the property. Hanging the curtains you have made can be left while more important matters are attended to.

Modifications

More modifications may be needed to the house then refitting carpets and having gas and electricity installations changed. Major work may be needed to satisfy the building society, or you may simply want to make modifications of your own. Much of this work is best carried out before you move into the property. You should consider this issue carefully before you decide to move in. Deciding factors will include the following items.

- Whether you can afford to finance the work immediately. You may have made allowances for the additional work in your mortgage. Many people undertake this type of work a little at a time when they can afford it and when they have lived in the house and got the feel of it.
- Whether you can afford the bridging finance to keep two properties on while work is undertaken.
- Whether you can cope with living with the in-laws, in a caravan parked in the garden, or can afford rented accommodation for a time.

The type of work which you might consider or have imposed on you by the bank or building society, along with other aspects of house alteration, is discussed in Chapter 9.

Completing the purchase

Completion day is the day all monies are handed over and a large scale game of musical chairs takes place as all the parties move from one property to another. While it would be far more civilised for this process to take place over a period of days, normally it is done on one day. Things can go wrong and properties may not be vacated at the appropriate time. These problems are not at your expense, however, unless you cause them.

Most of the banks and building societies send their drafts to your solicitor before completion day so that all monies can be handed over on time. On completion the deeds will be handed over to your solicitor along with your title to the property. If you are buying with a mortgage, deeds will pass to the bank or building society as security against the loan.

Moving

Your purchase contract will have set the date for the completion of the purchase. For most people this is also the date you move in. It need not necessarily be so, and in the case of long-distance moves which must be spread over more than one day, it cannot be. There can be major advantages in delaying the move into the new property by a few days so as to give you time to clean it out and get carpets and curtains fitted. If you are moving into a new house the delay may be forced on you because of hold-ups in putting the finishing touches to the house or flat. In these cases it will be necessary to put your belongings into store.

What this will cost depends on the precise nature of the move, the length of time in store and the quantity of goods involved. Normally the actual storage costs are only a small element of the total costs, so that once you have decided to store your belongings you might as well get as much work done as possible.

When enquiring about storage, check how the goods are to

be stored, in containers or loose. Many of the larger companies now use container storage which offers lower risks of damage and dirt, and also open storage. This involves far more movement for furniture which may be damaged as a result; open storage is often very dusty too, so it is wise to check conditions with the remover.

It is important to check that you are appropriately insured for removal and storage (see Chapter 7).

If you are moving some distance you might consider where you want the store to be located. Particularly if you are moving from south to north there are major cost advantages in hiring a northern rather than southern firm and storing near your destination. This also makes life easier and cheaper if you wish to take some goods such as carpets and cookers out of store earlier than the rest.

Professional or DIY removal?
Whether you use a professional remover or do the job yourself will depend on a number of factors:

- what funds you have available;
- the amount of furniture you have to move;
- whether you have any difficult items, such as pianos;
- how far you are moving;
- any access problems such as flights of stairs.

If you have only a few items to move and are reasonably fit, then hiring a van and doing the job yourself will save you money. Get several quotes for the van and check whether you will be charged mileage or not. An ordinary driving licence is valid for driving a van up to 7.5 tonnes laden weight.

Try to estimate the space you will need. It may be better to do several trips in a smaller van rather than one in a larger one. The distance of the move might decide this issue for you.

If money is an absolute problem then, clearly, doing the job yourself will be cheaper. However, if you cost your own time and accept that a removal company will employ people who are experienced, it often works out cheaper not to do the job yourself. You may find you will need specialist help on items such as pianos, in any case. If so it will cost little more to have everything moved for you.

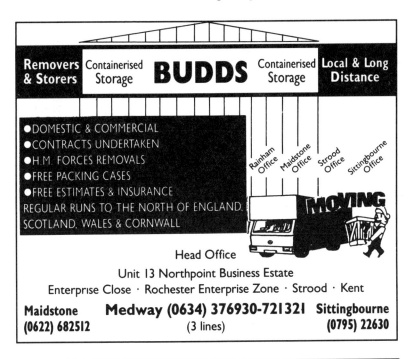

105

If you intend to use a professional removal company, names and addresses can be obtained from the British Association of Removers or Yellow Pages. Alternatively, consult friends and colleagues on which firms they have used.

Ask two or three companies to give you quotations. If a company quotes without visiting the property then you would be wise to discount them. A representative should visit you to discuss the service the company offers and to take details of the items to be moved. This is vitally important because there is no such thing as 'average' contents of a particular sized house. Books are a particularly deceptive item to move as they are very heavy for their bulk and hence necessitate more journeys to load. Removal men can spot vicars, teachers and lecturers by the number of books to be moved!

Discuss with the representative what you want to do and what needs to be moved. Do not forget the contents of sheds, lofts and greenhouses. If the shed is to go, most companies will dismantle, remove and reassemble. If in doubt – ask.

The cost will be based on either 1 or 2 plus 3.

1. The time it will take to complete the move. In this case you will be charged at an hourly rate for the hire of van and men. Check carefully what the rates are and whether they vary at different times of day or week.
2. The quantity of goods to be moved and the distances involved.
3. Any other services required. Many companies offer a packing and unpacking service as well as the provision of specialised containers for particular items.

When obtaining quotations, ask for different services such as packing and unpacking, laying of carpets and carpet cleaning, to be separately itemised. You can then decide which services you wish to include. It is important to obtain at least three quotations. You will be surprised how much they vary. Do not necessarily take the lowest quotation, however. Ask around to find out what the company is like before finally accepting the quote. Prices vary between different parts of the country, particularly because of variations in labour costs, so if yours is a longer distance move, obtain a quotation from a company in the destination area.

If funds are not limited, then have the remover both pack and

unpack all items other than those which you will need on the day of the move. This will take some of the hassle out of moving day and allow you to settle in very quickly. Some people even take a few days' holiday away from the move altogether and return to a completed job.

Remember that the representative will not see the property you are moving into. While visiting you, he will be able to assess any particular problems such as access, parking restrictions and difficult stairways at the existing house. You will have to inform him of any problems at the new house. This is particularly the case if you have large items to move, or are moving from a house into a flat, and if moving into a flat, which floor it is on.

Pre-sort your belongings

Moving house is a time when most people are forced to sort out their belongings and decide what they wish to keep and what should be discarded. To many, this is an extremely painful process, as throwing away even the least used item is a major challenge. If you are moving from a house into a flat or from a large to a smaller house, then this sorting out is essential. It is perhaps best to subdivide the surpluses into two groups, junk and saleable items. What goes into which category may be a matter of debate!

Everyone has their store of junk. Look in your loft, garage or shed and you will find it. It is important to begin the clear-out well in advance of the move, weeks if not months.

For saleable items several courses of action are possible.

- Sell through the small ads column in the local paper.
- Ask a dealer who specialises in house clearance to call and make you an offer. Get more than one dealer to quote.
- Ask at your local auction rooms whether they will handle the goods.
- Organise your own sale and advertise in the local paper.
- Take the items to a car boot sale.

Ask a local antique shop for advice about items of furniture which may have particular value. Do remember that most items have a value to someone, so think carefully before throwing anything away.

Any house move will unearth large quantities of items which no longer have a use or value. Offcuts of carpet bought years ago and kept 'just in case' in the loft, material left from curtains which you no longer use, offcuts from wood used in the last but sixth DIY job you did, are typical examples. Do not be tempted to take these items with you. Enquire of your local council whether they have a disposal service for such a miscellany. Most councils either provide a collection service or have large skips located at appropriate places, often council depots, which are open to the public. The skip system is very convenient for car owners and small items and quantities. It may be far more convenient to hire your own skip which can be left in your drive or on the road outside. In the latter case it is necessary to notify the police in case of obstruction or accident. Miniskips cost between £12 and £20 and larger skips between £25 and £30 each time they are emptied. This cost is soon covered by the sheer convenience gained.

Packing and labelling
If you are having your goods packed by the removal company they will arrive with their own boxes at least a day before the

move if a long journey is involved or early on the morning of the move for shorter moves. Many companies use different people for packing and moving. Arrange with the removers when they will come. Once they are packing you will need your survival kit!

If you are packing yourself, start as soon as possible. The removal company will supply you with cartons or boxes. Some use tea chests, often still containing tea! Make sure that you are supplied with enough cases. When packing boxes do remember that someone has to carry them. Save newspapers and other packing material well in advance. It is often useful to put a layer of heavy items at the bottom of a box with lighter ones on top. In this way you can use all the space available without excessive weight.

Label all boxes and items of furniture carefully indicating which room you want them to be put in. It might be useful to draw a sketch plan of each room in the new property to locate precisely where furniture will go. If you can beat the removal men to the new property, label each of the rooms themselves. If not you will be on constant call by the removal men to show them where to put things and unable to do other important things, such as sorting out the gas and electricity fitters or meter readers. If furniture is dismantled put all the fittings with the items, tied or taped on so they are ready when you begin to reassemble them. Similarly, tape picture hooks to the back of the pictures.

Carpets should be rolled and labelled. Label the underlay too. Piecing together underlay when you want to relay carpet is virtually impossible if it is not labelled. You will always find the vital pieces are missing. The removal firm will deal with all items of furniture, dismantling of beds etc. You will need to point out what is being left behind.

Electrical appliances

You should prepare major household appliances for the move the day before. The main items to consider are as follows.

- *Washing machine.* This will need to be disconnected from its fill taps. Usually this a straightforward job. Do remember that all washing machines and some spin dryers retain a small amount of water which will need draining before the appliance is moved. This is often achieved by lowering the outlet pipe to ground level and allowing the water to drain into a suitable receptacle.

● *Dishwasher.* This will be connected in a similar way to an automatic washing machine. The machine will contain water which should be drained before moving.

In both cases a suitable water supply and connections will be required at the new property. Even if the vendors have similar equipment, check that the connections are the same as those on your machines. Although a standard tap screw size has been accepted for plumbed-in appliances, there are many installations which still use other non-standard fittings. If you think that the fittings are wrong or there is no installation at all, arrange for a plumber to come and assess the job before the move if possible. If you have children, the loss of use of a washing machine even for a few days can be a nightmare.

● *Fridge.* This should be emptied and defrosted the day before the move, allowing time for any water to dry. Fridges which defrost automatically should be wiped out before moving.

● *Freezer.* It is possible to move without emptying and defrosting the freezer. Freezers are not very robust structures, however, and should not be carried more than one-third full. As you will normally want to empty and clean out your freezer once a year or so, it is probably far better to run stocks down and use this as an opportunity to clean it out. An empty freezer is far easier to move. If you wish to keep some of the freezer contents, ask a friend if you could use some space in their freezer for a few days while you move. You should run the freezer for a day or so before putting goods back in.

Both fridges and freezers can get airlocks in their cooling systems if tipped up. The ideal is to carry them horizontally or vertically depending on the type of appliance you have. If they have to be tilted then leave them for a few hours before switching them on again so that the air pockets can rise to the top of the system.

Children and pets

It was noted in the first chapter that children should be involved as much as possible in the house or flat purchase process. This is equally important in the move itself. While they may get in the way at times, children are usually very helpful if given their own specific tasks. Involvement will minimise any of their worries about moving. Most children, even the smallest, are aware that moving is an important event and will not want to be left out. Although some people farm their children out on the day of the move, the additional hassle which they may cause will be outweighed by their greater enthusiasm for the new house or flat. If each is given his or her own box to pack with toys at the old house, the emptying at the new can be an absorbing activity.

The pets will suffer the same uncertainties as the children. Somehow they sense that 'things are about to happen' and need equal care and consideration. If in any doubt about moving with pets contact your local RSPCA branch office.

On the day

Do not forget yourself. If you are not fortunate enough to have the benefits of a company move, the removal company doing absolutely everything while you are away for the day, then at least provide yourself with a minimal survival pack. Tea, coffee, a kettle, milk, sugar, biscuits, cake, sandwiches, soap, toilet paper, matches, a torch and all the appropriate telephone numbers should see you through the day. Take food for the new home if you will be unable to organise supplies or shopping at your destination. Remember that removal men appreciate a friendly customer who provides tea and biscuits or cake. It is a tiring, thirsty job even for the professionals. If the new home is distant or difficult to find, give the driver a clear map.

If the move is extending over two or more days you will need overnight kit as well.

When the removal van is loaded take a final look around the property to check that nothing has been left behind which needs to be taken and vice versa. Check that the meters have been read and that electricity, water and gas are turned off at the mains. Give the property a sweep out before you leave and try to leave it in the order you hope you will find your new property.

Not all vendors leave their property in the clean condition that you might hope for. Carpets and furniture cover many problems including large accumulations of dust and dirt. Once they are moved, major cleaning is sometimes required. Similarly, once a cooker is moved greasy grime is usually found behind and beneath. You may consider employing a contract cleaning company to give the property a thorough clean before the new occupants arrive.

The handing over of keys can be a complicated matter without prior planning. Make sure that you have found all keys to the property. In theory keys should not be handed over until the purchase or sale is completed and should be done by the solicitor. However, this can be extremely inconvenient even if the solicitor is local. Keys are frequently handed over by the estate agent or even the vendor. Many vendors will hand over one key at least so that the purchaser can get ready access. The other can be collected from the agent at a later, more convenient time. Avoid being caught waiting outside your new property with your removal company while someone goes off to find the keys. Delays of this kind, as well as adding to a stressful day, will also add to the removal bill.

At the new house, the unloading process should go smoothly if you have planned the operation carefully. If everything is labelled, leave the removal men to get on with the job and spend your time unpacking what is necessary for the first night. Make beds, put up curtains, unpack food, put the water heating on and connect up the fridge. These are the bare essentials. Do not expect the place to be ship shape in hours. You will find unpacked boxes everywhere and most flat surfaces covered with all sorts of the wrong things.

If you are fortunate to have a removal company which does not want the containers emptied immediately do not be tempted to empty all but the essentials on day one. Tip the men if you are satisfied with their work.

When the removal men have finished, check that the van is empty and that all is where you want it. If you do not have time to check everything before they depart, it is wise to record 'unchecked' on the job completion form that you will probably be asked to sign. This will cover you if you subsequently find damage has been caused during the move and you wish to make a claim against the company. Chapter 7 will deal further with insurance and associated issues.

Insurance and Related Issues

Your house or flat is probably the most expensive item you will ever buy and consequently you will need to consider insurance issues very carefully. Your building society or bank will also want to ensure that you have adequate insurance as it will probably have a major financial interest in both the property and yourself. Your property will contain all your personal possessions which themselves will need insurance cover. Indeed, there are many aspects of insurance which must be considered when buying and selling property. This chapter addresses the most important.

Insuring the structure

The bank or building society will insist that you take out insurance to cover the structure of your property and the fixtures and fittings. Many societies will send you insurance quotations with the mortgage offer. It is not obligatory to use the company which the society specifies but unless you have overriding reasons otherwise, it does make life simpler. The larger societies negotiate discounted rates with some companies because of the volume of business which they pass on. Flats will have structural insurance arranged by the managing agents or ground landlord, for which residents pay. If you are not buying with a mortgage, you must obtain suitable cover immediately yourself. Most solicitors now advise that this should be done on exchange of contracts, and it may in fact be required by the mortgage deed. Ask your solicitor.

Structural insurance covers a range of risks. It is important to realise, however, that there is some variation in the precise cover between different companies and policies. Do read the small print carefully and ask the company or the building society if you have any doubts. Most policies cover the structure, permanent fixtures, and fittings such as sinks, toilet and bath. Interior decorations are regarded by some as part of the building. Most policies cover garages but many exclude items such as sheds and greenhouses. Fences, gates and walls are often excluded. If you are buying a property with several out-buildings, a greenhouse or shed, check that they are covered.

The major risks which the policy should insure against are fire, lightning, storm and flood, explosion, earthquake, thieves, riot, aircraft and things falling from aircraft, falling trees, land-slip, collapse of aerials and water leaks. These risks include most of those which you might expect. Normally the cover is straightforward, but in some cases it can be problematic. For example, if a pipe bursts as a result of frost some companies will pay for the reinstatement of decoration etc but not the repair to the pipe itself.

Many companies include provision for the costs of alter-native accommodation for you and your family if the house is not habitable as a result of an insured risk until repairs can be carried out. This is a valuable additional element of cover. Do check the total sum insured in this context. The complete rebuilding of a property damaged, say, by fire can take several months. Temporary accommodation would be quite costly.

Most policies cover your liabilities towards third parties as a result of injuries to them or damage to property. The kind of risks are likely to include eventualities such as slates falling from your roof and damaging a neighbour's car.

Some policies also cover glass in doors and windows. Again, this element of a policy is particularly important if your new house has a lot of glazed doors, large picture windows or sealed unit double-glazed windows, all of which would be expensive to replace.

As in all insurance policies there are exceptions. Read the policy carefully to check what is included and what is not. If you do not understand the small print then ask your insurance company or broker. Some policies are still written in incom-prehensible language that many an insurance man does not understand. If in real doubt ask for your questions to be answered in writing. This soon clarifies the issue. If the policy excludes an item for which you need cover, then shop around.

Many policies have 'excesses'. These are the amounts which you will have to pay in any claim you make. For example, if you make a claim for £300 to replace the greenhouse blown down in a storm, your insurance company will deduct the 'excess' from the amount they pay you. If the excess is £50, then you will receive a cheque for £250. Excesses vary in amount between different companies and individual policies.

Some companies have two groups of policy, one with and one without an excess. Others include different excesses for different risks. Think carefully about the excess you accept. A policy which has no excess is likely to be more expensive than one with an excess. However, this additional cost may be very worthwhile. To give an example, if you live in an exposed location which habitually has strong winds, then you can expect a higher than average frequency of storm damage. The claims might be relatively small, £150 one year for repair of gutters, £100 for the replacement of tiles another. In this case a policy without an excess would be worthwhile.

One specific excess which all policies now include is that relating to subsidence, landslip or heave. As a result of major claims for subsidence in the very dry years of 1975 and 1976 most companies exclude a proportion of the rebuilding costs up to a fixed maximum. In parts of the country where underground workings are found, such as in coal mining areas, remember that the parties undertaking the workings (such as British Coal) are liable for any subsidence damage.

As with all insurance it is important to give careful consideration to the sum insured. This sum is the amount of money for which the property is covered and is the maximum which a company will pay out under any circumstance. It is crucial that the sum insured is adequate for the total risk. Companies use this as a guide for assessing liability on smaller claims. If, for example, your property is worth £80,000 but insured for only £40,000, and storms cause damage to your garage and outbuildings for which you claim £8,000, ie, one-tenth of the *value,* the insurance company will scale down the claim to one-tenth of the *insured value,* and offer £4,000. Many people realised this to their horror in the aftermath of the hurricane in the south of England in 1987. In this particular case, companies interpreted the proportion rule differently; some were strict, others more lenient. Do not assume that your company will be lenient!

One easy step to getting a mortgage

IF you're a first-time buyer or thinking about moving to a bigger home, are you finding mortgages confusing?

These days you can be granted a mortgage from several different sources, often presenting you with a bewildering choice ... Low-start, repayment, endowment, pension-linked, you name it.

Wouldn't it be easier by far to take the advice of real experts in the mortgage market? Here at Sun Life of Canada, we're ready and waiting to advise you how and where to get a mortgage, and just as important, we'll help you to get a good deal.

If you'd like to know more about mortgages, just fill in the coupon and return it to us, Sun Life of Canada, Department DM, FREEPOST, Basingstoke, Hants. RG21 2BR. We're here to help you.

YES! I'd like to know more about how Sun Life of Canada can help me get a mortgage. Please ask a representative to contact me for an appointment.   H P 017

Mr/Mrs/Miss _____

Address _____

_____

Postcode _____   Tel No. _____

SunLife of Canada

Established 1865. Sun Life Assurance Company of Canada. Incorporated in Canada in 1865 as a Limited Company. A Mutual Company since 1962. Sun Life Assurance Company of Canada (UK) Limited. Registered in England with number 959082. Registered Office: Basing View, Basingstoke, Hampshire RG21 2DZ. Members of the Sun Life of Canada Group of Companies which include also Sun Life of Canada Unit Managers Limited. Members of LAUTRO. Members of the Association of British Insurers.

It is vitally important to get the rebuilding cost of your property correct to ensure that the sum insured is adequate to cover the extreme eventuality. The cost of rebuilding is not the same as the market value; it can be considerably higher, particularly if non-standard building materials or methods of construction have been used. Costs also vary significantly in different regions of the country. A broad indication of reconstruction costs can be obtained from the Building Cost Information Service of the Royal Institution of Chartered Surveyors. As costs change rapidly make sure you obtain the latest figures.

Rebuilding costs will increase in line with other costs. Consequently it is vital to review the sum assured regularly to be sure it is in line with inflation. It is possible for this process to take place automatically by having an index-linked insurance policy. In this case the premium adjustments are made on the anniversary of the policy. Indexing is increasing in popularity. Even so, the correct indexed sum will still depend on:

- your informing the insurer of any changes to the property (extensions, garage, central heating etc); and
- the initial sum insured being accurate.

If you intend to make your own assessment obtain an up-to-date copy of the reconstruction costs tables and follow the procedure below.

- Measure the external floor area of your property and multiply it by two to take account of the first floor. If the property is on three floors it is usual to use a factor of 1/2 for the third floor.
- Add these figures together to give you the total floor area.
- Multiply this figure by the cost per square foot replacement cost as in the example on page 121.
- Add on the appropriate amount for garages. (Replacement costs for garages can vary between £2,500 for a single prefabricated structure to £7,000 for a large double garage in brick.)

Example

Large modern detached house south east England	
Total external area (includes upstairs)	2,000 sq ft
Rebuilding cost per sq ft	£40
Total cost	£80,000
Double garage	£7,000
Shed and greenhouse	£1,200
Grand total	£88,000

Index link by assuming at least an inflation level equivalent to the Retail Price Index. Better still, check each year with the Royal Institute of Chartered Surveyors on price increases in house building.

Do remember that in theory the responsibility for insurance changes hands on exchange of contracts. On that day the purchaser must provide cover. Many companies provide additional cover within the policy to include cover for the old and new property after the exchange of contracts up to completion. The length of cover varies but is usually three months, ample time for completion to take place in normal circumstances but something to keep in mind if there are delays.

If you are buying a flat, structural insurance cover is likely to be taken care of by the landlord who will include your proportion of the premium for the entire property as part of the service charge. In smaller flat developments the situation may not be so clear cut. If, for example, a house is subdivided into two flats without the establishment of a management company, the terms of the required structural insurance will be laid down in the deeds. The onus is then on the occupier to comply with the deeds. In these cases it is useful and usual for both occupiers to use the same insurance company. In this way you can ensure that the cover is identical and that both parties are equally protected.

If you are unfortunate enough to have to claim against your policy, get in touch with the insurance company as soon as possible. In the case of major disasters such as severe weather conditions the bigger companies set up special 'hot lines' to deal with claims.

Normally you should submit three quotations for the remedial work needed and wait for the insurance company to give you the go-ahead to have the work done. For small amounts, say, of £250 or less, the go-ahead will be automatic. For larger sums the company will use a loss adjuster to assess the damage and negotiate the level of payment. If they are particularly busy, companies may dispense with the use of a loss adjuster for larger sums too. Most companies will expect you to take immediate remedial action, such as putting up temporary cover on a damaged roof and will include the cost of this in the final settlement. It is after all in their interest that further damage is minimised.

Property cover is granted subject to reasonable maintenance being undertaken on the property. Insurance is not a way of financing much needed repairs. Loss adjusters do take the condition of the property into account when settling claims so it pays to maintain property as well as possible. If you make a claim and are not satisfied with the settlement it is worth arguing. If you are still unhappy you can contact the Association of British Insurers Consumer Information Department. They will advise you on the use of an impartial arbitration body which will consider your claim.

Specialist insurance

You may like to consider specialist cover for your property. The most common example of this is insurance against timber rot in its various forms. Companies such as Rentokil will insure property against these risks and will provide full reinstatement cover. Usually this cover is granted after the company has undertaken a full timber inspection whether or not treatment is needed. While this type of insurance is quite expensive the problems of wood infestation and particularly dry rot can be very expensive to repair. In older property the probabilities of some timber problems are quite high. This type of insurance, which is usually transferable with the sale of the property, is a very good selling point on older property.

Insuring the contents

After the structure the contents of the property are the next insurance item to think about. A bewildering array of policies is now available to cover household contents. Do remember during the purchase period to maintain cover at your old address until the move is over.

Contents insurance covers a wide range of house contents and personal effects including fixtures and fittings and decorations. Certain items such as valuable jewellery, musical instruments and bicycles may be covered up to certain values. Above that point additional cover is needed.

The risks which are insured against are similar to those discussed above for the structure, with the inclusion of theft.

Many policies provide additional cover for the contents while the owner is temporarily away from the property itself. Some companies provide a separate freezer insurance to cover you in the event of any failure in the electricity supply during your absence.

It is important to note that the cover discussed so far does not cover accidental damage on or off the premises. For this type of cover you need to consider an 'all risks' policy. This type of policy provides cover for accidental damage to clothing and personal effects as well as covering loss of money. Read the policy carefully, however, because some will provide useful additional cover in this section at no extra cost. If, for example, your family owns and uses several bicycles, then look for a policy which includes bicycles as part of the standard premium.

As you might expect there are exclusions in contents policies. Examine these carefully to ensure that they are not important to your particular circumstances. Look out in particular for replacement value or 'new for old' policies. Some companies have policies in which new for old is automatic. Others allow for normal wear and tear in the calculation of settlements.

For some risks insurance companies insist on individual items to be specified if they are valued at more than a particular amount. This is the case for example with musical instruments where cover usually extends to individual instruments of less than £250. This cover is fine for many instruments. It is far from adequate if you have a bassoonist or horn player in the family. The position of pianos is interesting as some companies include them as furniture. For others they are musical instruments. Do check.

Contents policies have excesses like other insurance. The excess does vary for different elements of the policy in many cases. Some excesses can be very high. Look out for policies with at most a £15 excess.

Choosing the cover you need can be difficult. Cost is the major determining factor. If you can afford a policy with an 'all risk' component in which premiums are acceptable and replacement values are available, then that is probably the best. Do look at the small print though to find out exactly what is covered. Many people have found to their dismay and cost at some time that a particular item was not covered or that the excess was so high that it made claiming pointless. If you have particularly valuable items, such as clocks or jewellery, ask directly whether they are covered and against what risks. If in doubt get the answer in writing from the company or broker.

Many people have difficulty in assessing the value of the house contents when they take out insurance cover. As the premium is calculated on the basis of the sum insured it is important to have adequate cover. If cover is inadequate then the company can refuse to honour the full value of any claim as in the case of structural cover. If you are ultra-efficient you will keep an inventory of all items you possess and will regularly add to this as and when you purchase items. Most people are not so efficient and resort to other methods of calculating values. Perhaps the best way of estimating values is to use a chart such as that shown in Appendix 6. For each room fill in the value of all the items assuming the replacement cost if you have a replacement policy and allowing for depreciation if not. (For some items such as clothes, full replacement costs are unlikely to be paid in any circumstances.) You may be surprised by the total figure you arrive at. Pay particular attention to carpets and floor coverings as these are frequently under-estimated when calculating the sum insured.

If this process of estimation is too onerous many estate agents can arrange for a full inventory to be taken and an insurance valuation provided. This may be a valuable course of action if you have particularly expensive possessions. You may have to provide professional valuations for specific items if they are to be covered separately in the policy.

Many policies now are index linked so that sums insured keep pace with rising replacement costs. The premium will be calculated in line with the new sum insured on the anniversary of the policy. The indexing of the sum insured does rely on the initial sum being correct and your notifying the insurance company of any changes in the contents to be covered.

Several companies now adjust the premium they charge to the risk involved, rather than simply calculating blanket figures. Two particular aspects of this practice are worth noting. The first relates to the area in which the property is located. Premiums are frequently loaded against inner city areas and the London area. The policy prospectus may define these areas in terms of groupings of post-codes. Unfortunately if you happen to live within one of these postal areas, you will have to pay the higher premium. It is worth shopping around, however, because not all companies follow this practice. The second aspect relates to the discounts which several companies now offer if certain precautions are taken against theft. These discounts work on a sliding scale depending on the level of protection you provide. If you are part of a Neighbourhood Watch, have installed additional catches on windows, have 'security locks' fitted to doors and have an alarm system then you can obtain as much as 20 per cent discount on the premium.

Insurance cover during removal and storage

It is important to ensure that the contents of your home are insured while in transit and store. Even the best removal men have occasional accidents. Cover can usually be provided by the removal company or through your own household contents policy. The premium for storage is usually based on the period of time in store. Check that the cover is adequate and does not contain exclusions with which you are unhappy. Some removal companies automatically include insurance cover in their quotation. If they do, ask to see what cover this gives. If in doubt take out separate cover.

Insurance associated with mortgages and finance

Mention was made in Chapter 5 of various aspects of insurance which are directly related to the financial side of home purchase. This section looks at these in a little more detail.

Mortgage protection policies are designed for those who take out a straight repayment mortgage which has no life insurance associated with it. In the event of the death of the insured the mortgage is paid off. Such cover is usually quite inexpensive. The sum insured usually reduces as the life of the policy progresses in line with the decreasing level of outstanding capital owed. If both husband and wife's incomes are important to the repayment of the mortgage, it is wise to consider cover for both parties.

Temporary payment insurance. You may consider the eventuality of being unable to repay your mortgage because of ill health or unemployment. It is possible to insure against these events although the premiums can be quite high. As with all insurance, there is a wide variety of cover. Some policies only cover repayments over a maximum of 24 months, others exclude certain types of employment. If you are considering this type of cover read the details very carefully.

Mortgage indemnity cover. If you borrow more from a bank or building society than is their normal rule, 95 per cent of the value of the property rather than the usual 90 per cent, for example, the lender may insist on suitable cover for the additional 5 per cent. Some lenders require indemnity cover for advances over 70 to 75 per cent. Frequently this is done by taking out indemnity cover. In the event of your being unable to repay the mortgage and the property being sold, the insurance company will guarantee the lender any part of the loan outstanding if the sale price is less than the purchase price. Premiums for this type of cover are usually paid as a lump sum. Cover will normally be arranged by the lender.

Paying for insurance

Insurance premiums for all types of cover are increasing all the time and can cause some hardship when the renewal notice arrives. There is always the temptation in such cases to lower the level of cover rather than face the higher premiums demanded. For many people insurance premiums bunch at one time of year, often associated with the timing of the last house move. Most companies now offer the opportunity of paying by instalments over either four or 12 months. Payment can usually be made either by standing order or direct debit arrangements with your bank. In this way your insurance costs are spread out during the year. If you wish to make use of this facility, examine the charges made for this service carefully. Some companies make no charge, some add a percentage of the premium.

Chapter 8
Selling Your House or Flat

Many of the issues involved in selling your house or flat will have been discussed earlier in reverse when we discussed the process of buying. You will have learned a lot about showing people around the house, for example, by your own experiences as a prospective purchaser. Similarly you will have realised the importance of being clear as to what is included in the sale and what is not. Nevertheless, it is important to consider the selling of property systematically and it is to this issue which we now turn.

Using an agent or doing it yourself

Which of the two approaches you take when you sell your property will depend largely on time and money. An agent will save you time and will cost you money. If the local housing market is buoyant DIY selling is often very successful. If the market is sticky, the resources of an agent are often worth paying for. The DIY method will entail you in the valuation, advertising, negotiation and agreement process which the agent would undertake on your behalf.

If you are buying locally through an agent, it is often advisable to sell your property through the same agent. In this way the agent has an increased financial interest in the transaction and is likely to put a special effort into the sale.

The DIY approach

The first question to resolve is 'How much do I ask?' for the property. There are several ways in which you can arrive at an answer.

- Look at the similar properties nearby which have recently been on the market. Do not forget to add in an inflation factor.
- Look at properties in the area with similar characteristics, numbers of rooms etc, which are for sale or have been recently sold. Remember that precise location can influence price.
- Ask for an estate agent's valuation. Most agents will undertake a market valuation at no charge in the hope that they will gain your business. Do emphasise that you are not instructing the agent to sell the property but getting some idea of its value prior to sale.
- Instruct a surveyor to give you a market survey. It is often a good idea to commission a partial structural survey. While there will be a charge for this (see Chapter 3), a survey report will both identify any problems in the property and will be an attractive sales tool. It will give you a good idea of how much bargaining you might anticipate and accept from prospective purchasers.

The asking price will be related to several factors (see Chapter 1). Do not be tempted to be greedy and ask significantly more than the norm for the area or the valuation you are given. What you may gain financially you will probably lose in the longer period the property is on the market. The exact price you ask may have a psychological effect on potential purchasers; £6.99 sounds a lot less than £7; similarly £99,000 sounds far less than £100,000. There are acceptable thresholds for prices in different areas for different types of property. If you price your property above the threshold it will sound expensive.

The price will be influenced to some extent by what is included in the sale and the general condition of the property. The final agreement of what you leave will be made between you and the purchaser. In deciding what to take and what to include it is useful to consider three simple questions.

- What items do I definitely require for the new property? This will depend on what you are buying and what the vendors might be leaving. If your carpets are reasonably new and will fit rooms in the new house then take them. The same goes for curtains, curtain rails, cupboards etc.

- What items could be used at the new property but would not be ideal? Could I sell them as additional items to the basic sale price of the house?
- What items will be of no use at all? These might as well be part of the sale.

Everyone likes to think they have got a bargain when they buy anything. The inclusion of some items in the sale can often encourage a purchaser. Fitted carpets which cannot be used at the new property might as well be included. If you are moving into a house with a fitted kitchen where your top loading washing machine will not fit, you might consider including that in the sale. The resale value of washing machines is very low and is not worth the effort of investigation.

If you are selling items outside the asking price of the property itself, take care to pitch your price appropriately. Greed may lead you not only to lose the sale but to have the problems of disposal too. Make a complete list of what is included and what is not. Those items which are for sale separately should be priced on a separate list. A list such as that in Appendix 4 will both help the purchaser and avoid subsequent misunderstandings.

As a rule when you sell a house you should include all fixtures unless otherwise agreed. The definition of what is a fixture can be a little difficult in some cases, such as with fitted furniture. The commonsense test relates to whether removal of the item would cause major damage to either the structure which would have to be made good, or the item in question.

The general condition of a property can be important to its sale. Poorly decorated houses are more difficult to sell than those in good order, and fetch lower prices. If you redecorate before selling, keep the scheme neutral, as many buyers will redecorate to suit their own taste when they move in.

Where do I advertise?
There are several approaches which you can take. You may decide to use all. Much will depend on the amount of money you are willing to spend. Do not be tempted to take the least cost approach to advertising for, as a rule, the more you spend the more effective your advertising will be.

Newspapers

Most newspapers, local, regional and national, have property pages. These are usually on a specific day of the week, often Saturdays. Normally you will advertise in the local or regional press although if you have property which might be in national demand you might consider the national press. For property in London and the South East the national press might be appropriate as it might for secluded cottages in the Highlands or Central Wales.

Rates vary considerably between papers. Discounts are often available for multiple or series bookings. If the property is sold before the series is completed you will receive a refund on cancellation.

Before you use a specific paper ensure that it is appropriate for your property. You should then work out the format of your advertisement. There is a great deal of skill involved in advertising copywriting. There are accepted abbreviations for use in such advertisements. Some of these are shown in Appendix 8. While they will save you money, abbreviations tend to devalue what you want to say. Look in the press to make your own judgement. Flowing, flowery prose makes a property sound more attractive. Emphasise the strong points about the property and play down the weaker ones. Your advertisement must bring people to look at the property. If it does not sound attractive, it will not sell. Examples of newspaper advertisement copy are given in Appendix 8.

A photograph will make a significant impact on your advert. The cost need not be prohibitive especially if you are taking a series of adverts.

'For Sale' boards

The 'For Sale' board method can be a very effective way of advertising your house, less useful for flats where it is difficult to identify the particular property concerned. Most house-hunters will drive around a neighbourhood at the outset of their search, if not later, getting a feel for the area. The 'For Sale' board is bound to catch their eye. Boards are particularly good for weekend househunters passing by.

Most good hardware/DIY stores sell suitable notices for this purpose. Do take care not to annoy your neighbours with the location of the sign you use nor the local authority planners

with its size. There are restrictions on the size of advertisements you can use without first having planning permission.
There are some problems associated with boards.

- Passers-by will learn your telephone number from the
  board and may use it for criminal purposes.
- You may find difficulty in controlling potential purchasers
  calling in without warning.

Shop display method
Many people advertise their property sales in a variety of 'shop'
situations from the local supermarket or cornershop, where
there may be no charge, to the property centres set up by
solicitors. These centres link the shop display principle to
conveyancing. There is a charge for such services which is
usually related to the selling price of the house. (Full details of
this approach can be obtained from the National Association
of Solicitors Property Centres.)

Whichever of the above approaches you adopt it will be useful
to provide a simple brochure containing details of the property
and sale for prospective purchasers. Not only will such a
brochure help to answer many of their questions, it will remind
them of the property itself when they come to draw up a short
list of prospective properties. You can get the style of such a
brochure from the example given in Appendix 8. Be sure to
include any positive attributes about the property which are not
visible to the visitor such as wood treatment insurance cover,
recent rewiring and existing planning permissions as yet not
carried out.

The estate agent approach

Selling through an estate agent has many advantages over the
DIY method especially if you are busy and would find being
available to show people around difficult. Agents usually have
a very wide publicity network and hence can offer excellent
advertising for your property. Most people looking for property
will visit an estate agent at some stage of their search. The
agent will show prospective purchasers around the property if
necessary. Many will arrange mortgage facilities for specific
properties subject to the status of the purchaser.

Although in a period of high demand for housing when property sells very easily, many people feel that an agent does not 'earn' his fee, it is probably still useful to involve an agent.

As there are a large number of agencies now established, deciding which to commission can often be bewildering. Several factors are worth keeping in mind.

- Personal recommendation of friends or colleagues.
- Size of the practice and the access the agency has to wide advertising and publicity news-sheets.
- The qualifications of the staff. Most reputable agencies will be staffed by members of the Faculty of Architects and Surveyors (FAS), the Incorporated Association of Architects and Surveyors (IAAS), the Incorporated Society of Valuers and Auctioneers (ISVA), the National Association of Estate Agents (NAEA) or the Royal Institution of Chartered Surveyors (RICS).
- Ability of the agent to see the sale through to exchange of contracts.
- The type and location of property with which they normally deal.
- Whether the agency is selling the property you wish to buy.

You may ask several agents to give you a valuation of the property before commissioning one to sell for you. Many people choose the agent who gives the highest valuation for the property. In many cases a lower valuation is the hallmark of a more realistic agent who knows his clients and the local market well.

Normally one of the agent's staff will visit the property to establish the market value and discuss the asking price with you. To establish the valuation he will measure all the accommodation and take details of features of each room in preparation for writing the selling brochure. He will need details of items which are not visible by inspection but which will be important to the sale. Such items will include cavity and other insulation, recent major repairs and rewiring, rates, any service charges and ground rents and outstanding planning permissions. The agent will then produce a brochure to mail out to his applicants.

135

Most agents will discuss with you the approach to selling that they will take, whether they will accompany applicants to the property, the level of newspaper advertising they will use etc. Do remember that you are commissioning the agent to act on your behalf. If you are unhappy with anything he suggests, say so.

The agent will charge a fee for his services. Some charge a flat rate, some charge a percentage of the final sale price. Make sure that you know what method is being used and get a firm estimate in writing of the costs. Some agents make additional charges for services such as 'For Sale' boards and advertising. Check what these charges are likely to be and set cost ceilings in writing. Advertising charges can soon escalate out of control. Do not accept the first quotation for selling the property. Shop around and negotiate the fee. It is usually possible to get a reduction in the fee if you are persistent.

You can commission more than one agent to sell the property. In this case establish in writing the terms on which each agent is dealing with the sale. Take care that all agents do not charge you the selling fee.

Showing viewers around

Whichever method of sale you adopt you will have to get used to answering enquiries and showing people around. You may be able to get the agent to take some of this work off your hands although in this case you will have to leave a key with the agent. Normally the agent will contact you to arrange appointments.

It is impossible to keep a property immaculately clean and tidy in anticipation of potential purchasers visiting. Especially if you have children, you have to accept that it will always be a little untidy. Some aspects are worth paying attention to however. Keep the windows reasonably clean, the lawns cut and paths swept. Watch out for smells too. If you are fond of curries or have very young children, an air freshener would be a good idea!

You will soon get into the swing of showing people around the property. Show them each room, describing what is there and answering any questions. When you have completed the tour, suggest that they look around on their own. People are often reluctant to talk about features of a property with the

vendor in the background and appreciate a few minutes on their own. Making one's mind up about a property is a major decision and one which is often based on a relatively brief visit. When the prospective purchaser has had a chance to look around, be prepared for questions.

Questions will range from the costs of heating, the rates and the neighbours to details of what you are including in the sale. Be honest in your answers. Serious misrepresentation in the final approved contract could find you fighting a damages claim.

Everyone has his or her own approach and manner when viewing a house which makes separating the interested from the rest very difficult. Deciding to whom you will sell is an art in itself. There are some obvious rules of thumb, but in the end it is advisable to keep a property on the market until the contracts are exchanged. Similarly, do not allow the agent to place an 'Under Offer' or 'Sold' sign up.

Things to ask of your potential purchasers will include:

- The current position of their own house sale. Is it on the market? Has a purchaser come forward? It is sold?
- The financial position. Is a mortgage available? Have they a mortgage certificate?
- When do they want to move?
- Is it a company move or not?

Dealing with offers

Do not necessarily sell to the purchaser who offers the highest price. Negotiating on the price will be done by your agent who will consult and advise you on the best course of action. If you are selling yourself then you will have to negotiate. Very rarely does a purchaser offer the asking price outright. In these cases you should suggest that you will consider the offer and get in touch when you have had a chance to consider all the offers. How far you take the bargaining process will depend a lot on how long the property has been on the market. In the first few weeks you can afford to wait, unless of course the price offered is only a few hundred pounds less than you hope for.

Once the offer is accepted, the purchaser's building society or bank will be instructed to undertake a valuation survey.

Because of the expense involved, few purchasers will commission the valuation survey until their offer is agreed. A full structural survey may also be commissioned. In both cases you must be prepared to give access to the surveyors involved. Both these surveys may lead to the purchaser returning to negotiate the agreed price. If the survey has found problems it is advisable to discuss their impact on the purchaser's offer. You then have three options.

- Lower the price.
- Undertake to rectify the problems.
- Sell to another party.

In taking the last course of action, remember that the faults are likely to be found by another surveyor who visits the property. They will not go away and hence it is frequently inadvisable to terminate the deal.

On accepting the offer, your agent will contact your solicitor to get the sale procedure into motion. If you yourself are selling the property you should contact your solicitor or conveyancer giving full details of the agreed sale, the name and address of the purchaser, his solicitor, the agreed price and full details of all items included in the sale.

Once a sale has been agreed, most purchasers will want to look over the property, take measurements and generally take stock of what they are purchasing. You should give them reasonable access. They may also want trades people to visit to give estimates and take measurements. Again a reasonable attitude should be taken. Do not let yourself be inconvenienced too much, however. The sale is unlikely to fall through on this account.

Auctioning your property

It may be more appropriate to sell your property by auction rather than by private treaty. Auctions are usually used for property sale where the market value is uncertain, where the property is of an unusual type or where the property is part of the estate of a deceased person. The objective is to let the market and bidding establish the best price.

As many estate agents are also auctioneers, discuss the appropriateness of an auction for your property. An auction will cost you approximately 2½ per cent of the agreed price so that it can be considerably more expensive than the normal way of selling. If the auction does not realise the reserve price, the minimum price which you are willing to accept, you may have to pay a fee rather than the commission. Establish these points in writing before the event.

The agent will usually advertise the auction widely for several weeks before the event. Newspaper adverts and posters are used. As these can be expensive and will be charged for at cost, you should agree an advertising budget with the agent.

As with any house sale, potential bidders will want to visit the property and be shown around. Building society valuers and structural surveyors will need access to carry out their work. The presence of surveyors will give you a useful indication of the level of interest in the property.

During the pre-auction period you may receive offers for the property. You should insist on the auction being subject to the condition of 'unless previously sold', so that you can accept an offer in this way.

Once the auctioneer's hammer has fallen, the buyer is committed to buy the property and pay a deposit of 10 per cent to the auctioneer. Contracts are signed there and then with a completion of the purchase within four weeks.

Whichever way you sell your property, you can learn a lot from your own experiences as a buyer. Remember that buying is a major decision and that the buyer is frequently at the mercy of his agents during the process. Once you have found a buyer in whom you have confidence, have patience. Do not put unnecessary obstacles in the way of your purchaser and give as much assistance as he requires to complete the deal successfully.

Selling in Scotland

As noted in Chapter 4 the Scottish house sale and purchase process differs in certain ways from that in the rest of Britain. These differences are outlined as they relate to property sale.

There are three ways of selling property in Scotland:

- the DIY approach;
- selling through a solicitor;
- selling through an estate agent.

In each case you will need to involve a solicitor at the outset so that he can make appropriate checks on the deeds and undertake searches in anticipation of a binding contract being made by a purchaser. When using an estate agent he is most likely to pass all offers on to your solicitor before you make a decision on which to accept.

You will establish the price for the property as described in the earlier sections. Normally offers are made above the asking price and so you may be advised to pitch your asking price below what you expect to achieve.

When finally deciding which offer to accept it is usual to set a final closing date for offers. After that date you will decide which offer to accept. As you are not obliged to accept the highest figure the factors discussed earlier on which offer to accept will be useful.

If the property is owned by more than one person, consent for the sale must be given by all parties. For married couples who do not jointly own the property, the Matrimonial Homes (Family Protection) (Scotland) Act of 1981 requires that the non-owner partner grants permission before the sale can take place.

When you have agreed which offer you will accept, the purchaser's solicitor will prepare the offer and submit it in writing. There will then follow discussion of the terms of contract and 'Missives', the legally binding contract. These matters take only days to complete and are one of the strengths of the Scottish system. There then follows the examination of title deeds, the preparation of the disposition (the document which transfers the title of the property) and other formalities such as arranging mortgage payments. The disposition is then handed over to the purchaser's solicitor in return for full payment of the agreed purchase price.

Your solicitor will then send you an itemised statement of the entire transaction and the balance of the sale after the various parties involved have been paid.

Chapter 9
Modifying and Extending Property

Whatever house or flat you finally decide to buy, there may be modifications which you would like to undertake. Alternatively, there may be modifications which you could make to your own house or flat which would remove the need for a move in the first place. This chapter examines some of the factors involved in house modification and extension. It begins by looking at some of the 'settling in' jobs before moving on to larger scale extensions.

Settling in jobs

There will be a wide rage of such jobs which might include:

- plumbing;
- electrical fitting and wiring;
- decorating;
- fitting alarms;
- extending the telephones.

Plumbing

The most likely plumbing jobs you will encounter will be the installation of an automatic washing machine and dishwasher water supply, the replacement of tap washers and problems associated with the central heating system.

In all cases you will need to locate the stop taps for the various water supply networks in the property so that you can isolate the item which needs attention. In modern property, there will be two stop taps for the cold water supply, one outside the property and one inside. You may need to use a little detective work to locate them. The outside one may be in the pavement while the inside one is most likely to be on the supply pipe under the kitchen sink. The same is true in some older houses. However, if the system has been modified you may have to search. (If in doubt ring the local office of the Water Board. They will usually send someone out to locate the taps.) The stop tap for the hot water is usually located on the outlet pipe from the supply cistern in the roof space.

The central heating system will have a similar stop tap. In this case it will be found around the heating water reservoir in the roof space.

Locate all these taps as soon as possible after you move in. You may need to turn off the supply in an emergency. If you undertake any plumbing work allow a minute or two for water to drain out of the system before starting work.

Most plumbing jobs are within the capability of the good DIY person. If suitably accessible pipes are available, the modern 'plumbing in' kits for washing machines and dish-washers make this task possible for most people.

Plumbing and drainage are subject to Building Inspector approval. The local water authority are responsible for the approval and occasional inspection of all water fittings. If you are making major modifications you would be advised to consult them.

Major plumbing tasks which you may consider in the longer term will include:

- replacement of bathroom and kitchen fittings;
- modifications to the central heating system;
- replacement of lead pipes (in older property).

If you need a plumber for any reason consult friends and neighbours about who they use. If you have problems finding a suitable tradesperson, the Institute of Plumbers will provide you with a list of plumbers in your locality. Before you call a plumber out check the obvious. If the problem is with the heating, check that the boiler is lit, the electricity is on and the radiators are not just full of air and in need of bleeding.

Electrical fittings

In general electrical installations are best left to qualified tradespeople. Your structural survey may have commented on the state of the electrical system. If the house is over 30 years old it is wise to have the wiring tested. This work can be undertaken either by the electricity board or a private contractor.

If the property is inadequately provided with sockets you may need additional ones installed. Again this is normally work for a specialist as connections will have to be made into the main fuse box.

There will be some small scale electrical jobs, however, that you can undertake yourself. These will include the fitting of new wall lamps to existing circuits, replacing old ceiling roses and wires and even the replacement of light switches. In all cases the mains electricity must be switched off.

Whether you intend to undertake any electrical work or not, it is useful to locate the electricity master switch. You may need to turn off the power in an emergency!

Decorating

A coat of paint and new wallpaper will soon transform your new house or flat into your home. Painting and decorating is perhaps the most popular of the DIY activities too. When you buy your new property you should give careful thought to what decorating needs to be done as opposed to what would be nice to do. Do not be tempted to undertake more than what you can reasonably cope with! Painting and decorating is far easier in an unoccupied house so give some thought to doing the work before you move in. If you are employing tradespeople you should find this cheaper too in an unoccupied property.

Before you begin work consider carefully what other jobs you are likely to do in the property and try to phase them accordingly. If for example the house needs rewiring or attention to the roof, have each of these done before you begin decorating.

Alarms and security devices

We mentioned in Chapter 6 that many insurance companies now offer discounts for properties which have anti-intruder devices fitted. Now is the time to consider fitting such devices to your property. The local police crime prevention officer will visit your property and advise you free of charge on what is needed. Window catches and security locks are easily fitted by the DIY person or local tradesperson. Burglar alarms are the domain of the expert. The National Supervisory Council for Intruder Alarms will be able to give advice and a list of recommended installers.

While considering this type of equipment, you would be strongly advised to consider the installation of smoke detectors. There are many DIY models on the market.

Telephones
Many households now like to have more than one telephone in the property. As long as there is already a British Telecom plug-in type socket you can make use of the many DIY extension kits which are on the market to install your own system. Alternatively, BT or a qualified electrician will do the work for you. If you do not have a telephone already installed contact BT as described in Chapter 5.

Major works

The jobs discussed above are seen as immediate, to be under-taken within weeks of moving in – or before if possible. This section considers a range of other work which includes both remedial work and modification. This is not intended as a DIY manual to house maintenance but rather a discussion of what work to consider, how to undertake it and what benefits it will bring.

The benefits
When considering major work on a property you should ask yourself three simple questions.

- *Is the work essential?* This may be measured by the work being a condition of the mortgage. In this case the work *must* be done. Types of work included in this category will be attention to the roof and installation of a damp-proof course.
- *Will it improve living conditions significantly?* You may consider that the installation of central heating, double glazing, a new kitchen or bathroom would make life more

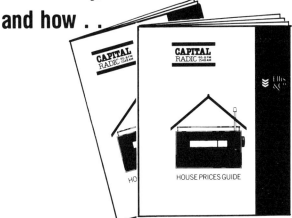

comfortable or an extra room or bedroom would give you the extra space you need.

● *How much will it cost?* It is important to consider costs against the additional cost you would incur if you were to move to a new house or flat and the effect on the value of the property both now and in the future.

The answers to the first two questions are straightforward. The building society may not give the full loan until the work is undertaken. If double glazing, central heating or another room would make life better, then do it. It is when you come to issues of cost that you should give very careful consideration to the work to be done. Put plainly, most home improvements are a waste of money unless you intend to stay in the property for several years. The notion that you are putting value on the property may be true, but only in the long term and in some circumstances not even then. Only undertake improvements if you will get immediate benefit from them.

There are one or two exceptions to this general rule. These include garages, central heating and possibly double glazing. Even in these cases you will recover only part of the total construction costs after two or three years. The likely expected percentage of construction costs recovered after two years varies between specific modifications as follows:

Garage	60–70 per cent
Central heating	45–70 per cent
Double glazing	45–70 per cent
Extra bedroom	10–30 per cent
Kitchen extension	10–30 per cent

These estimates are based on the full professional costs of required work done and will be more favourable if you do the work yourself.

Most estate agents will advise strongly in favour of moving house rather than extending your existing property. The reasoning is based on the fact that there are prevailing prices in different residential areas and to take a property out of that prevailing price range by extension will not have a corresponding effect on selling price. It may be the case, however, that by extending your property you bring it up to the prevailing

MAIN&MAIN

Head Office:
198 Finney Lane
Heald Green
Cheshire
SK8 3QA
Tel: 061-437 1338/9

Branch Offices:
59 Church Road
Gatley, Cheadle
Cheshire
SK8 4NG
Tel: 061-491 3634

90 School Road
Sale
Cheshire
M33 1XB
Tel: 061-962 6721/2

Regal Buildings
Marsland Road
Sale Moor
Cheshire M33 3HQ
Tel: 061-962 6821/2

409 Stockport Road
Timperley
Altrincham
Cheshire WA15 7XR
Tel: 061-980 6838

SOUTH MANCHESTER'S LARGEST INDEPENDENT ESTATE AGENTS
FOR ALL YOUR PROPERTY REQUIREMENTS

price. This might happen, for example if you are considering adding a fourth bedroom to a property in an area in which most houses already have four bedrooms.

It is also important to remember the other costs involved in buying and selling property which might substantially effect the actual cost of moving. If the cost of a kitchen extension is £6,000 and the costs of purchase and sale are £2,500 then the net cost is only £3,500. In addition, take into account the hassles involved in buying and selling. Although turning your home into a building site can be stressful, it is almost certainly less so than moving.

If you are in any doubt about the effect of extension or modification, seek the advice of a local estate agent.

Raising finance

Many of the aspects of finance discussed in Chapter 5 are relevant to home extension and are only mentioned here.

Mortgage

Building societies and banks will usually extend your existing mortgage for extension and other developments to property. To qualify for tax relief the developments should in theory be permanent.

In the unlikely event of your existing lender being unwilling to extend your loan, you could consider taking out a second mortgage with a different society or bank for the additional amount. Alternatively, you might settle your existing loan and take out a completely new mortgage for the old and new amounts together. While this may seem an unnecessarily complicated way of financing the development and one which will incur costs such as solicitors' fees, it may allow you to shop around and obtain a more competitive interest rate. Extending the mortgage is usually the cheapest way of financing an extension.

Personal loans

Most banks and a range of credit houses will offer loans for home improvements. In most cases the maximum length of the loan will be five years. For periods greater than five years and for large amounts security may be required. Interest rates may be fixed for the period of the loan, removing the uncertainties of interest rate fluctuations from your calculations.

Getting work done

The way in which you get the work done will depend on several factors including the complexity of the job, your own DIY capabilities, the amount of free time which you have to devote to the work, disposable income and ability to raise finance. You may decide to undertake part of the work yourself and engage a tradesperson for the rest. A typical example of where this approach may be used is in the extension of a kitchen.

Work undertaken	Tradesperson	Self
Ordering of materials		*
Excavation and footings		*
Roof	*	
Brickwork	*	
Glazing		*
Plastering	*	
Electrical	*	
Plumbing		*
Fitting units		*
Painting		*
Floor covering		*

If you adopt this approach you must programme the work carefully so as not to interfere with the tradespeople.

If you intend to employ a contractor there are two principal approaches which can be taken.

- Select a firm which will undertake the entire project for a fixed fee. The names of such firms can be obtained from the Federation of Master Builders, the Institute of Plumbing and the Electrical Contractors Association. Alternatively you can turn to Yellow Pages.
- Manage the project yourself and engage tradespeople to undertake the various elements of the work. This is frequently the way a contractor will organise the work himself, so you will save the 'middleman costs'. This method can save considerable amounts of money although you should anticipate the work taking longer. If the work you are undertaking is complicated it may be worth employing an architect or building surveyor. In this case he or she will advise you on contractors and will manage the work. There are no set scales of fees for this type of work so it is useful to obtain more than one quotation.

Getting permission

There are two main permissions which you may require before you can undertake your development, planning permission and Building Regulations consent. While neither need cause any problems, there are occasions when you simply cannot do what you would like. In these circumstances you should think seriously about moving house or flat.

Planning permission

The planning system is intended to ensure that any new development fits in with its surroundings and does not unduly affect your neighbours. Many small scale developments associated with individual housing are, however, exempt. Check with the local authority planning department at an early stage.

'Permitted development', ie that which does not require permission, includes:

- increases in the volume of the property up to 70 cubic metres or 15 per cent of the original volume in England and Wales and 50 cubic metres or 20 per cent in Scotland;
- conservatories and porches;
- garages;
- loft conversions as long as the conversion does not increase the volume of the house.

Interior work does not require permission nor do a variety of smaller external developments. The requirement in specially designated areas such as national parks and conservation areas differ from these general rules and you should contact the local planning office for advice.

Your planning application should be accompanied by copies of plans of the proposals and a fee of £33. The plans can be drawn up by yourself or you can engage a draftsperson to do them for you. If you engage a contractor, he will draw up and submit the plans on your behalf. It is unlikely that your plans will be turned down, particularly if you have discussed your proposals before submitting them. If they are turned down you have the right to appeal. However, in most circumstances when small extensions are not permitted, you would be well advised to reconsider the proposals.

Do not be tempted to do any work without consulting the planning authority. They have the power to enforce their will and can require you to restore the property to its original state. This may prove very embarrassing and expensive!

Two useful booklets, *Planning permission: a guide to householders* and *Planning appeals* are published by the

Department of the Environment and are available free from local council planning departments. The Royal Town Planning Institute also produces a series of useful leaflets, available free from the Institute.

Building control

The building regulations are intended to ensure that buildings are structurally sound. Approval must be obtained for most development work to property both internal and external. There are some exceptions:

- carports open on two sides, porches and conservatories no greater than 30 square metres in area;
- detached buildings such as garages provided that they are not used as bedrooms and are less than 30 sq m.

Normally building approval is gained by submitting full plans along with the appropriate fee to the local authority officers. Following approval, the officers will inspect the work at its various stages of completion. You must notify the building control officer when the work has reached the appropriate stage so that it can be inspected.

What kind of development to consider

Loft conversion

Loft conversions are a very popular way of gaining an extra bedroom, play-room or study. They make use of redundant space in the roof void. In older property such a conversion is relatively straightforward as roof pitches and structure allow a clear area of adequate ceiling height. In modern property, the roof trusses frequently require major modification to the roof structure itself before the loft can be developed. A quick glance into the roof void will tell you whether the job is possible or not.

Ceiling joists are unlikely to be strong enough for the new floor and will need strengthening or replacing. Access to the space may be a major problem. While in England and Wales a loft ladder is adequate, in Scotland a staircase must be fitted. In this case valuable space is lost and costs rise considerably.

Modern roof lights provide a simple and economical form of window and do not need planning or building regulation permission. Dormers are more costly and require building regulation permission.

Kitchen or other ground floor extension

This type of extension can either be prefabricated or conventionally built. There are many off-the-shelf extensions on the market. Even a small extension can make a suprising difference to the feel of space in a kitchen.

Ground floor developments of this type usually do not require planning permission but may raise difficulties with building control, particularly if the proposed extension covers existing drains or gas and electricity pipes and cables.

Converting a garage into a room

This is often a very satisfactory way of extending your property, particularly if you have an integral garage and space to erect a new one. In many cases a new internal access, window and floor is all that is required to create a new room of ample proportions.

If the garage is attached rather than integral the ease of conversion will depend on the garage structure, in particular whether it is built with cavity walls or not.

Two-storey extensions

If you require a considerable amount of additional space then you might consider a two-storey conversion, which may incorporate a study, play-room, bedroom and bathroom. There are two major problems with this type of extension.

- The internal layout of the property could mean that access to the extension is difficult and may actually lose you space. A former bedroom may have to become a corridor for example.
- The size of the property may become out of keeping with surrounding property and this may reflect in the resale value of the property.

What extensions cost

It is very difficult to generalise about the cost of extensions because the precise specifications will have a major effect on cost. The cost given below are for guidance only.

Type of work	Cost £
Loft conversion	8,000 – 12,000
Kitchen extension	9,000 – 11,000
Garage conversion	5,000 – 7,000
Two-storey extension	16,000 – 20,000

These figures can be approximately halved if you do the work yourself and reduced by 10 per cent if you pay the tradesperson promptly in cash. In addition there are significant regional variations in both materials and labour costs. If you live in Greater London you can expect to pay some 15 per cent more than the average, while in the South West you should find costs 10 per cent or more less than average.

Whether to go ahead with any major modifications will depend on the answers to the earlier questions. It is important to weigh up costs against total property valuations, changes in property values and the costs of moving. If you intend to add an extension costing £10,000 to a property valued at £120,000, then the proposition is probably worthwhile financially. If on the other hand the £10,000 extension is on a property valued at £25,000, you would probably be advised to consider moving.

The final decision may rest on whether you can better cope with the stress and trauma of having builders and mess around or the stress of moving.

APPENDICES

Costs of Installing and Running a Heating System

Detached house (Household of five. Floor area 104 square metres)

Heating system	For system £	Running costs per annum	
		£	£
Oil	2,193	638	490*
Solid fuel	1,777	370	294
Mains gas	1,678	455	362
Electricity	1,649	530	385

Bungalow (Detached. Household of two. Floor area 67 square metres)

Heating system	For system £	Running costs per annum	
		£	£
Oil	1,819	470	390*
Solid fuel	1,714	270	230
Mains gas	1,304	348	296
Electricity	1,204	370	289

Semi-detached (Household of four. Floor area 89 square metres)

Heating system	For system £	Running costs per annum	
		£	£
Oil	1,873	495	392*
Solid fuel	1,662	377	311
Mains gas	1,358	364	299
Electricity	1,522	383	284

Older terraced house (Solid walls. Household of four. Floor area 88 square metres)

Heating system	For system £	Running costs per annum	
		£	£
Solid fuel	1,657	424	407**
Mains gas	1,473	392	378
Electricity	1,408	402	380

Post-war terraced house (Household three. Floor area 79 square metres)

Heating system	For system	Running costs per annum	
	£	£	£
Solid fuel	1,547	305	274*
Mains gas	1,304	301	266
Electricity	1,209	296	245

Two-bedroomed flat (Middle storey, two external walls. Household of two. Floor area 61 square metres)

Heating system	For system	Running costs per annum	
	£	£	£
Solid fuel	1,489	226	214*
Mains gas	1,237	216	192
Electricity	853	170	135

Note
1. Systems are either water-filled radiators or night storage heaters.
2. Costs include any standing charges
3. * denotes cavity wall insulation is installed.
   ** denotes draught proofing.

Source. A Guide to Home Heating Costs. Midlands and North. Energy Efficiency Office. Editions of this booklet are available for the Southern Region, Wales and Scotland from the Central Office of Information.

Useful Addresses

Association of British Insurers
Aldermary House
Queen Street
London EC4N 1TT
01-248 4477

Association of Licensed Conveyancers
200–201 High Street
Exeter EX4 3EB

Association of Relocation Agents
Springfield House
Aston Tirrold
Oxfordshire

Black Horse Agencies
(Chainmaker)
11–15 Monument Street
London EC3R 8JU

British Association of Removers
277 Gray's Inn Road
London WC1X 8SY
01-837 3088
Send large stamped and addressed envelope
with postal enquiries.

British Chemical Damp Course Association
16a Whitchurch Road
Pangbourne
Berkshire RG8 7BP

British Insurance Brokers' Association (BIBA)
BIBA House
14 Bevis Marks
London EC3N 7AT
01-623 9043

British Rail Property Board
274-280 Bishopsgate
London EC2M 4XQ

British Wood Preserving Association
150 Southampton Row
London WC1B 5AL
01-837 8217

Building Employers Confederation
82 New Cavendish Street
London W1M 8AD
01-580 5588

Central Office of Information
Hercules Road
London SE1 7DU
01-928 2345

**Corporation of Insurance and
Financial Advisers (CIFA)**
6–7 Leapale Road
Guildford
Surrey GU1 4JX

Council of Licensed Conveyancers
Golden Cross House
Duncannon Street
London WC2N 4JF
01-210 4603

Department of the Environment (Housing)
Victoria Road
Ruislip
Middlesex HA4 0NZ

English Heritage
Fortress House
23 Savile Row
London W1X 2HE
01-734 6010

The Faculty of Architects and Surveyors
15 St Mary Street
Chippenham
Wiltshire SN15 3JN

Federation of Master Builders
33 John Street
London WC1N 2BB
01-242 7583

Historic Buildings Bureau for Scotland
New St Andrews House
St James Centre
Edinburgh EH1 3SZ

Historic Buildings Company
PO Box 150
Chobham
Surrey GU24 8JD

Homequity
(Goldlink Chainsaver)
Bridge House
Farsnby Street
Swindon SN1 5BG

**The Incorporated Association of Architects
and Surveyors**
Jubilee House
Billing Brook Road
Weston Favell
Northampton NN3 4NW
0604 404121

**The Incorporated Society of Valuers
and Auctioneers**
3 Cadogan Gate
London SW1X 0AS
01-235 2282

Institute of Plumbing
64 Station Lane
Hornchurch
Essex RM12 6NB
Hornchurch 72791

Law Commission
Conquest House
37 St John Street
London WC1N 2BQ
01-242 0861

The Law Society
113 Chancery Lane
London WC2A 1PL
01-242 1222

Law Society of Scotland
26 Drumsheugh Gardens
Edinburgh EH3 7YR
031-226 7411

The National Association of Conveyancers
2–4 Chichester Rents
Chancery Lane
London WC2A 1EJ
01-405 8582

The National Association of Estate Agents
Arbon House
21 Jury Street
Warwick CV34 4EH
0926 496800

National Association of Plumbing, Heating and Mechanical Services Contractors
6 Gate Street
London WC2A 3HX
01-405 2678

National House-Building Council
Bedford House
Bedford Street
Belfast BT2 7FD

National House-Building Council
Chiltern Avenue
Amersham
Buckinghamshire HP6 5AP
0494 437477

London Office (for information)
58 Portland Place
London W1N 4BU
01-580 9381

National House-Building Council
5 Manor Place
Edinburgh EH3 7DH

National Inspection Council for Electrical Installation Contracting
Vintage House
36–37 Albert Embankment
London SE1 7UJ
01-582 7746

National Supervisory Council for Intruder Alarms
Queensgate House
14 Cookham Road
Maidenhead
Berkshire SL6 8AJ

New Homes Marketing Board
82 New Cavendish Street
London W1M 8AD

Northern Ireland Office
Department of the Environment
Stormont
Belfast 4

Prudential Property Services
(Chainbreaking)
Winchmore House
Fetter Lane
London EC4A 1BR

Royal Institute of British Architects
66 Portland Place
London W1N 4AD
01-580 5533

Publications
Finsbury Mission
Marchand Street
London EC1V 8VB

Royal Institution of Chartered Surveyors
12 Great George Street
London SW1P 3AD
01-222 7000

Royal Town Planning Institute
26 Portland Place
London W1N 4BE
01-636 9107

Save Britain's Heritage
68 Battersea High Street
London SW11 3HX
01-228 3336

Scottish Office
New St Andrews House
St James Centre
Edinburgh EH1 3SZ

Society for the Protection of Ancient Buildings
37 Spital Square
London E1 6DY

Welsh Office
Cathays Park
Cardiff CF1 3NQ

Appendix 3
Sitting Tenants: The Right to Buy

Landlords from whom you have the right to buy

Group 1
District Council
County Council
London Borough Council
Common Council of the City of London
Council of the Isles of Scilly

Group 2
Inner London Education Authority
Metropolitan county police authority
The Northumbrian Police Authority
Metropolitan fire and civil defence authority
The London Fire and Civil Defence Authority
Metropolitan county passenger transport authority
The London Waste Regulation Authority
The West London, North London, East London and Western
Riverside Waste Disposal Authorities
The Merseyside and Greater Manchester Waste Disposal
Authorities
The London Residuary Body
A metropolitan county residuary body

Group 3
A new town or urban development corporation
The Commission for New Towns
The Development Board for Rural Wales

Group 4
A housing association if registered with the Housing Corporation as
long as it is not a charity, a co-operative association or has not

received public funding
The Housing Corporation

Other public bodies, tenancy with whom counts towards qualifying period and discount

Area electricity boards
Fire authorities
Government departments (excluding prison officers' accommodation)
Internal drainage boards
Parish councils
Passenger transport executives
Police authorities
Water authorities
Agricultural and Food Research Council
British Airports Authority
British Broadcasting Corporation
British Gas Corporation
British Railways Board
British Steel Corporation
British Waterways Board
Central Electricity Generating Board
Civil Aviation Authority
Electricity Council
Lake District Special Planning Board
London Regional Transport
Medical Research Council
National Bus Company
National Coal Board
Natural Environment Research Council
Nature Conservancy Council
Peak Park Joint Planning Board
Post Office
Science and Engineering Research Council
Sports Council
Trinity House
United Kingdom Atomic Energy Authority
Community Councils in Wales
National Library of Wales
National Museum of Wales
Welsh Development Agency
Commissioners of Northern Lighthouses
Countryside Commission for Scotland

Highlands and Islands Development Board
North of Scotland Hydro-Electric Board
Scottish Special Housing Association
Scottish Sports Council
South of Scotland Electricity Board
Education and library boards in Northern Ireland
Fire Authority for Northern Ireland
Northern Ireland Electricity Service
Northern Ireland Housing Executive
Northern Ireland Transport Holding Company
Police Authority for Northern Ireland

Appendix 4

Checklist of Fixtures and Fittings Included in the Sale

The following list provides a basis on which to record those fixtures and fittings being included in the sale. For each room tick the items to be included.

Room 1
Curtain rails, tracks and fittings
Curtains
Blinds
Pelmets
Carpet
Wall fittings such as mirrors and shelves (specify)
Furniture (specify)
Heaters
Light bulbs and shades
Other fitted electrical apparatus such as clocks and fans (specify)
TV aerial and fittings

Room 2 etc
As above

Bathroom
Towel rail
Toilet fittings
Cabinet
Mirrors
Shaver fittings
Curtain/Blind
Carpet
Heater
Medicine cabinet

Kitchen
Cupboards (even those which are apparently fitted)
Utensils
Cooker
Built-in appliances (specify)
Curtain/Blind

Outside
Greenhouse (and associated equipment)
Sheds
Fuel store
Trees, shrubs and flowers
Garden equipment (such as swings) and garden furniture

Others
Fuel oil or solid fuel
Residual building materials
Paints, door bells

Who to Inform of Your New Address

Money Matters
Bank
Building Societies
Pension, Benefit (including Child Benefit)
Inland Revenue
National Insurance/DHSS
Saving Certificates and Save as You Earn schemes
Premium Bonds
Shares (company secretary), Stockbroker
Credit card companies
Hire purchase companies
Local business accounts (newsagent, department store, laundry etc)

Insurance
Broker or agent
Life insurance
Household insurance
Car insurance
Private health insurance
Other risks

Car
Registration authority
Driving licence
Motoring organisation

Personal
Friends and acquaintances
Doctor
Dentist
Landlord (if applicable)
Tenants (if applicable)

Other health advisers (homoeopath, chiropodist, optician)
Clubs and societies
Children's clubs and societies
Associations or clubs on whose mailing list you are included (mail order firms, concert and theatre bookings)
Libraries
Other subscriptions (book club, wine club)
Schools
TV Licence Records Office
Employer
Professional organisation and trade union
Motoring organisations
Gas, electricity, water, telephone, post office services

Appendix 6

Calculating the Value of the Contents of Your Property

Obtain a proposal form from your insurance company. They will usually have their own checklist. Otherwise, use the following table to estimate the value of contents room by room. You can extend the table to include all rooms and spaces in the house and gardens. Rooms and spaces to include are: lounge, dining room, kitchen, hall, stairs, landing, main bedroom, bedrooms one, two, three . . . bathroom(s), toilet(s), cloakroom, utility room, garage, conservatory, sheds and other outbuildings.

Checklist

	Lounge	Dining room	Kitchen etc	TOTAL
Carpets, rugs, floor covering				
Furniture				
Soft furnishings				
Televisions, videos, audio equipment				
Household appliances				
Cooking utensils and provisions. Cutlery				
Valuables				
Leisure equipment, musical instruments				
Garden furniture, paint, tools				
Household linen				
Clothing				
Other items				

TOTAL £

175

Appendix 7
Mortgage Comparisons

Loan: £50,000 over 25 years

Joint application

Age of applicants: 40 years

Interest rate: 10.25 per cent

	Type of mortgage		
	Repayment £	**Low cost endowment** £	**Full endowment** £
Capital/ Interest	467.90	427.08	427.08
Less tax relief	45.19	64.05	64.05
Mortgage protection	29.50	—	—
Endowment premium	—	81.50	200.00
Net cost	452.21	444.53	563.03
Projected bonus	None	24,000.00	171,350.00

(Assumes available tax relief is all at the standard rate of 25 per cent)

Appendix 8
How to Advertise

1. Items to include in advertisement

Type of house
Age
Type of construction (brick, stone, render)
Location
Number of rooms
   Bedrooms
   Reception
   Bathrooms
   Kitchen
Type of heating
Insulation and double glazing
Garage
Garden
Other outbuildings (sheds, greenhouse)
Tenure (freehold, leasehold)
Price

Emphasise any of the above items which are particularly good selling points. In a pre-war house note if the house is rewired. In older property note any special treatments such as damp course or roof timbers.

2. Advertising copy shorthand

If you look through the property sections of the press you will soon discover the shorthand used in many adverts. They do save money but to the unfamiliar can be quite incomprehensible.

CH	Central heating
FH	Freehold
GR	Ground rent
clk	Cloakroom

c&c	Carpets and curtains
det	Detached
f&f	Fixtures and fittings
gge	Garage
lge	Large
rm	Room

3. Model advertisement

Stone built 1920s detached house in well stocked gardens. In popular part of town with excellent schools and access to local shops. Ten minute walk to local station. Four double bedrooms two with en suite shower. Family bathroom. Two WCs. Cloakroom. Laundry. Kitchen recently modernised with Aristocrat units. Gas central heating, double glazed to all main rooms, cavity insulation. Large garage with additional parking space. Excellent decorative order throughout. Offers region £144,000. Tel . . . . . .

4. A typical seller's brochure

A well planned detached freehold residence offering spacious yet easily managed accomodation close to local schools and shops and within easy walking distance of the village.

Photo

Address

The property, which is constructed of brick, with a rough cast finish and tiled roof, is in a highly sought after residential area. It is within a few minutes' easy walking distance of both Ilkley and Ben Rhydding, both of which are well served with commuter train services to Leeds and Bradford.

The property has good sized gardens to all sides most of which are laid to lawn. Mature trees and hedges create seclusion and privacy to the south facing gardens.

The property has been extensively modernised in recent years including a new gas-fired central heating system, en suite facilities in the main bedroom, and play-room and office above the garage. The roof has been extensively refurbished in the last 12 months including the replacement of valley gutters. A full Rentokil wood infestation insurance policy covers the timbers. A Rentokil chemical damp course was installed approximately six years ago.

The property is completely double glazed and has a generous distribution of 13 amp power sockets.

The accommodation includes:

1. Arched covered porch with glazed and panelled entrance door with glazed side panels.
2. Entrance Hall. 16 ft × 6 ft. Understairs storage cupboard with fitted shelves, quarry tiled floor, double central heating radiator. Telephone point.
3. Cloakroom. Pedestal wash basin, coat hooks. Seperate WC. Wall tiling.
4. Through Lounge. 20ft × 15 ft. With stone fireplace and incorporating a recessed ornamental niche. Baxi open fire. Copperad Minivector heater, double radiator, plaster cornice, wall lights and double multipaned French windows to south facing patio and garden.
5. Dining Room. 19ft × 14ft. Attractive recessed shelf unit, two double radiators, wall lights. Telephone point.
6. Kitchen-Morning Room. 14ft × 20ft. Wide range of Hygiena wall and floor units, working surfaces and wall shelving. Central heating boiler and controls. Plumbing for both dishwasher and automatic washing machine. Xpelair wall extractor fan. Tiled walls. Multi-panelled French door to patio. Door to entrance porch.
7. Rear Entrance Porch. 4ft × 4ft. Glazed door to side of property.

FIRST FLOOR
1. Main Bedroom. 19ft × 15ft. En suite facilities including Mira shower and wash hand basin. Large floor to ceiling fitted wardrobes and cupboards. Windows to south and east.
2. Bedroom. 12ft × 14ft. Wash basin and tiled splashback.
3. Bedroom. 10ft × 14ft. Fitted cupboards and airing cupboard with insulated hot water cylinder.
4. Bedroom. 8ft × 9ft. Door to:

5. Play-room. 12ft × 4ft 6ins. Skylight window, fitted shelves and fitted desk space.
6. Family bathroom. Modern avocado suite. Fitted shower unit. Tiled walls.

SECOND FLOOR

1. Bedroom. 7ft × 16ft (max). Unusual shaped room with Ventalux roof light and south facing window. Integral bed. Range of fitted cupboards.

OUTSIDE

1. Detached double garage. 19ft × 20ft, incorporating:
   Separate laundry with stainless steel sink and plumbing for automatic washing machine.
   Play-room. 13ft × 12ft.
   Study/office. 8ft × 13ft. Fitted desk and shelving.
   Telephone point.
2. Aluminium greenhouse 12ft × 8ft.
3. Brick and render garden and coal store.

The property has large gardens, drive and parking space for several cars and separate hard standing for a caravan.

Rateable Value: £350. Rates payable in 1987/88 £1,062.

Space and water heating costs approximately £700 pa.

All services are available and the electricity supply is currently installed to use the 'Economy 7' tariff.

Additional fixtures and fittings, carpets and some curtains can be purchased at extra cost subject to negotiation.

PRICE £98,500 subject to contract.

For your information our solicitors are:

XXXXXXXXXXXXXXXX
XXXXXXXXXXXXXXXX
XXXXXXXXXXXXXXXX
Tel: XXXXXXXXXXXX

Contact: Ms S Brown

If you wish to view the property or discuss further details please telephone John or Mabel Smith on 0888 765432.

Index of Advertisers

Addison & Co 69
Alexander Reid & Frazer 65
Allied Property Sales 83
Anil Khanna & Co 51
Bevan Ashford 54
Bishop's Move 105
Blythe Liggins 63
Bowens 57
Brain Sinnot & Co 55
Budds Removers & Storers 105
Butterworth Insurance Brokers 117
Castle & Jordan 65
Charles Reynolds & Associates Ltd 109
Charles Rosenberg & Co 48
Clement Gallagher Mortgages & Pensions 83
Clifford Cowling 48
CMG Carlton Retirement Planning Ltd 79
Colin Blackmon 135
Crawters 39
C W Estates 87
Dalzell & Co 137
David Goulding & Co 61
Dickson Child & Green 60
Ellis & Co 147
Ellis Fowler Belcher 55
Fox Brooks Marshall 72
Girlings 49

Gordon Brown 57
Harrison-Groves 59
Harvey & Marron 71
Hirst Williamson 67
Hollinshead & Co 59
James Fernley & Partners 81
Jordans 53
Kenneth G Nicklin & Associates (Life) Ltd 117
Lambeth Building Society 92
Lancasters 137
Main & Main 149
Mander Hadley & Co 61
J Nicholas Mellor 69
North Wales Mortgage and Investment Centre 87
Pink & Jones Ltd 107
Wm F Prior & Co Ltd 71
Property Matters 107
Rossendale Investments 85
Segan & Co 63
Slater Hogg Mortgages 91
Solicitors Property Centre 53
South Coast & Metropolitan Insurance Services Ltd 88
Stelrad Doulton Ltd *back cover*
SunLife of Canada 119
Thomas C Sutton & Co 67
Whitegates 135

Index

advertising 131-3
  boards 132-3
  newspapers 132
  shops 133
alterations, major 146-54
  considerations 146-8
  raising finance 150
asking price, selling 129-30
assessing needs 17-31
assistance (home improvement) 42-3
auctioning property 139-40

bank 52, 78
  informing of move 99
borrowing limits 89-93
boundaries 70
bridging loan 72, 97
building regulations 153
building societies 52, 75-8
  informing of move 99
bungalows 23

capital gains tax 93
central heating 20
  electric 21
  gas 20-21
chains 97-8
  breaking 97-8
children 112
completion 72, 103
  date 72
condition 34
contract of sale 68-72
  exchange 62
conversion to flats 43
conveyancer 52, 64, 66, 72
conveyancing 64-72
  DIY 64-6
council house, purchase of 31
curtains and carpets 102

damp, surveys for 38-9
decorating 145

deeds 103
deposit 52, 72, 94
detached houses 23
draft contract 68-70

electrical appliances, removal 110-11
electrical fittings, modification 145
estate agents 29, 133-6
  choice of 133
  Scotland 73
exchange of contracts 70-72
extensions
  cost 155
  type 154

financial considerations 43-6, 75-97
  first-time buyer 94
Financial Services Act 94
fires
  electric 22
  gas 21
  open 22
flats 23-4, 35-7
freehold 26
freezer, moving of 111

garage and car parking space 19
garage conversions 154
garden 19, 34
gazumping 62
grants 42-3

heating 20-22, 34
house prices 12-13
  influences on 14-15
housing market 12-15
  control of 15

inspection 33-9
insurance 98
  amount insured 118-21
  claims 121-2
  contents 122-5
  during removal and storage 125

mortgage insurance 125-6
payments of premium 126-7
specialist 122
structure 115
insurance companies (mortgages) 78

keys, handing over 113

labelling 109-10, 113
Land Registry 66
layout 34
lease 36
leasehold 26
legal process 64-73
loans 80
    for alterations 150
location 25-6, 34
loft conversion 153-4

mail, redirection of 100
maisonettes 23-4, 35-7
meters, reading of 112
modifications 102-3
mortgage applications 52, 94-6
mortgage brokers 80
mortgage certificate 94, 138
mortgage indemnity cover 126
mortgage protection policies 125-6
mortgage, refusal of 96
mortgages 75-96
    for alterations 150
    builders 78-80
    choice 89-90
    employers 80
    endowment 86-8
    local authority 78
    low-cost endowment 86-8
    pension 88
    repayment 82-6
    special schemes 92-3
    unit-linked 89
moving date 103-4

Neighbourhood Watch 125
new homes hot line 30

offer
    dealing with 138-9
    making an 47-52
older property 28
    purchase of 42-3
ownership
    advantages/disadvantages 10-11
    changing pattern 11-12

packing 109-10
pets 112
planning permission 152-3
plumbing 143-4
press 29-30
property
    bungalows 23
    detached 23
    flats 23-4, 35-7
    new 26-7
    older 42-3
    semi-detached 23
    size 17
    terraced 22

rates 45, 98-9
rebuilding costs 120-21
'red lining' 96
removal 104-13
    who does it 104-8
risk 8
rooms, number of 17-19

Scotland
    procedure in 73-4
    selling property 140-41
    solicitors 73
searches 66
    fees for 68
second-hand property 27-8
security 145-6
selling
    DIY approach 129-33
    estate agent approach 133-6
semi-detached houses 23
service charges 45
services, for flats/maisonettes 36
services (gas/electric)
    informing about move 101-2
signing contract 71-2
sitting tenants 31-2
situation 34
size 34
solicitor 52, 64, 66-72
    Scotland 73
stamp duty 66
storage 103-4
stress 8-9
structural assessment 37-8
structural problems 42
surveys
    structural 39-41
    valuation 52-8

tax relief 80, 88-9, 93
telephone 100-101, 146
terraced houses 22-3
'title' 72

uncertainty 8

valuation report 56
valuation survey 52-8
    fee 52-6
visits to inspect property 34-5

wood treatment surveys 38-9